PEN THE SWORD

THE UNIVERSAL PLOT SKELETON OF EVERY STORY EVER TOLD

ADRON J. SMITLEY

Copyright © 2018 Adron J. Smitley

All rights reserved.

0 6 2 1 1 8

Digital ASIN: B07F37YL2G

Print ISBN: 978-1721783083

For free articles on everything plot, character, and story structure architecture please visit:

adronjsmitley.blogspot.com

also by Adron

fiction (fantasy)

<u>Soothsayer Series</u>

Veilfall

Jinn

Powerless

Godzai
(*title pending/novel forthcoming)

<u>Non-Fiction</u>

On Writing Well

Punching Babies: a how-to guide

Pen the Sword: the universal plot skeleton of every story ever told

CONTENTS

*	THE CORE ELEMENT	1
STAGE 1	OLD WORLD STASIS	Pg # 17
STAGE 2	NEW WORLD FLUX	Pg # 24
STAGE 3	THINGS COME TOGETHER	Pg # 29
STAGE 4	FALSE VICTORY	Pg # 36
STAGE 5	THINGS FALL APART	Pg # 46
STAGE 6	FALSE DEFEAT	Pg # 50
STAGE 7	FALSE SOLUTION	Pg # 57
STAGE 8	TRUE RESOLUTION	Pg # 60
**	THE MASTER PLAN	Pg # 64

RECOMMENDED READING

On Writing Well
by Adron J. Smitley

Techniques of the Selling Writer
by Dwight V. Swain

The Story Solution: 23 Actions All Great Heroes Must Take
by Eric Edson

Creating Character Arcs
by K. M. Weiland

* THE CORE ELEMENT

Every story ever told, every movie ever filmed, every novel ever written follows the universal plot skeleton in this book. Because it's the most logical yet dramatic process to resolving a life-changing issue newly encountered. And when things come down to it that's what all stories are about, right? Someone striving to resolve a life-changing issue they have never dealt with before which ultimately ends in triumph or, less often, tragedy. Either a major problem or a big opportunity. A world-breaker or a world-saver. A whopper of a doozie.

You say you failed your driver's test because you forgot to signal? So what. I failed mine because I drove over an old lady—after crashing through a school bus full of blind nuns!

You say you got a pay raise at work? Big deal. I just inherited $100 million smackaroos and a haunted mansion to boot!

Dwight V. Swain, author of *Techniques of the Selling Writer*, said it best. And I'll paraphrase. All stories contain one fundamental desire when you break them down to their absolute bare core. The protagonist seeking to obtain or achieve one of three outcomes above all things else:

1. *Possession of* something.
2. *Relief from* something.
3. *Revenge for* something.

As the writer, this is where you begin. This core element not only tells you the beginning of your story but also its ending, and all in three little words.

Once you know the fundamental element of your story you then know its core. And once you know its core you won't be led astray because every scene must in some way revolve around this one core element. If it doesn't then it belongs in a different story. This core element is the reason why your story exists and why you need to tell it. Without this core element there is no story. Period.

So how do you know which of the three is your story's core element? That depends on your Inciting Incident (a.k.a. the Catalyst). Because the Inciting Incident creates the reason why your protagonist seeks Possession of, Relief from, or Revenge for *something*.

I can see you're anxious for an example so I'll give you one.

Let us say murder is your Inciting Incident. You don't yet know how or why or to whom, all you know is murder tickles your muse and you want to start from there. So let's keep it simple with plain old-fashioned hammer-to-skull murder. Bundles of conflict all snarled up into one simple word.

You've already made your first decision because the Inciting Incident is either a major problem or a big opportunity, and murder is obviously a major problem.

Now you have three options—Possession, Relief, Revenge—but a whole plethora of roads to travel.

Maybe your protagonist wants Revenge for a murder committed against a loved one because lawful justice won't satisfy their aching thirst.

Maybe they want to gain Possession of necessary evidence to convict the murderer in question because the police are morons who couldn't plug their bungs with their own thumbs.

Maybe they witnessed the crime and are now being stalked by the murderer and seek Relief from the chase.

Or maybe they committed the murder themselves in the heat of passion and . . .

See how easy that was?

As soon as you choose a particular Inciting Incident you immediately have at least three options to pick from which then begins branching your untold story into an endless array of possibilities.

With murder as the Inciting Incident you have a beginning because obviously you have to set things up before the murder. Then comes the murder itself, which mucks things up for everyone involved—especially the victim! Then, and depending on the circumstances of the murder, you decide which course of action your protagonist takes. And whether possession, relief, or revenge . . . you now have an ending because your protagonist either achieves said possession, relief, or revenge or they don't.

Pantsers take note because this is where you come in. Don't like knowing the end of your story before you get there? Of course you don't because you're a Pantser! You enjoy not knowing until you actually write it.

And that's perfectly fine because nobody says you must know the ending. Just because you choose possession, relief, or revenge as your "ending" doesn't actually make it so. What this does is allow your Pantsing muse wiggle room to create that wonderful unexpected twist ending all readers enjoy.

You have an idea of what might happen and so plant inviting bread crumbs along the way to lead your reader along as well as your self.

Everyone assumes your protagonist is going to eventually obtain or achieve their desired possession, relief, or revenge—then BAM! you hit them upside the head with a twist ending they never expected because you never expected it until you wrote it yourself!

Possibilities spilling all over the place. Watch your feet!

Your protagonist gets their revenge at long last then BAM! they find out their victim was also a victim who was blackmailed into the murder by a serial killer.

Or your protagonist gets their relief from the hunt then BAM! only to find the murderer isn't dead or in prison after all but is now their new mailman or neighbor and nobody but them is the wiser.

Or your protagonist gets their possession then BAM! the evidence also places them at the scene of the original crime as an accomplice and they're locked away with the murderer as their new cell mate. "Grab the bunk, punk, 'cause you're serving booty duty!"

But maybe you haven't decided on a particular Inciting Incident just yet.

Okay. Let's work backwards instead of forwards.

What kind of ending do you want, triumph or tragedy? Does your protagonist gain possession of, relief from, or revenge for something?

Let's choose possession, and not in the literal sense for this example. You want a happy ending with your protagonist getting the girl of his dreams. If he has her at the end then at some point he didn't have her because he hadn't met her yet. Or maybe he did but lost her by becoming a gambling drunk. Or maybe she was his best friend's girl and . . .

Do you see where I'm going with this?

Plot doesn't place restrictions, it offers opportunities.

How about another example for the sake of fun?

Your protagonist seeks relief from something. How about debt? Debt sucks, and everyone's had it at one time or another so it's relatable. For your protagonist to be in debt she first needs be out of debt. So now we have a beginning with your protagonist living a happy-go-lucky life owing nobody nothing. Everything's hunky-dory. She moves out of her parent's house with a bright future ahead, takes a chance and spends her entire savings as a down payment for a big loan on an expensive new car to ensure she has a dependable ride to work every day. But that's okay because her first paycheck will cover her bills.

Then the Inciting Incident happens because we need to put the protagonist in debt. She's on her way to work in her new car when BAM!

she's sideswiped and her poor car sits in twisted ruins. Delirious, she's pulled from the flaming wreckage and . . .

No, that's not "good" enough. An Inciting Incident is life-changing. World-breaking. So let's really pile it on her with a major problem.

She's driving to work in her new car . . . after a night of partying with her friends while celebrating moving out from her parents' house and being on her own for the first time. But she drank too much so she's chugging coffee to sober up while taking back roads hoping no cops spot her erratic driving. And praying her new boss doesn't notice the bags under her red eyes or the smell of skunk beer on her breath or—BAM! she swerves to miss a giant pothole and BAM-BAM! runs over an old lady crossing the street!

She gets out. Nobody's around. She blisters the air with a string of Hail Marys about the huge dent in the hood of her car then panics at all the blood. So she dumps the old lady in her trunk like a sack of dog food and peels away. Drives to the secluded place where star quarterback Jimmy Fourhands tried to take her virginity back in high school after prom, pops her car in neutral and pushes it into the lake where it disappears in a bubbling plunge.

Now she has no car, no way to work, is a murderer, and she still has to pay off her loan on the car rusting at the bottom of Lake Humpsalot.

Oh wait. She can just claim someone stole her car. Perfect! That'll excuse her from paying off the loan while explaining her lateness to work.

Too bad she spent every last dollar on the car loan and couldn't afford insurance.

It's important to remember that the Inciting Incident happens *to* the protagonist.

I'll use The Matrix as an example.

What is the Inciting Incident of The Matrix?

The movie opens with agents attempting to chase down Trinity so they can get to Morpheus because only Morpheus has the access codes to the last human city, Zion, uncontrolled by the machine overlords. Trinity is talking to Cypher about Neo while watching Neo, and the agents tapped the phone line and zeroed in on her position. They chase Trinity down in an epic action opener but she gets away by the skin of her teeth. Only now the agents know Neo's name, something they didn't know before.

Without this key piece of information discovered, nothing in the rest of The Matrix would happen as it does. If the agents didn't find out

Neo's name by tapping the phone line then they would never seek Neo out to use him to get to Morpheus, so this must be the Inciting Incident, right?

Wrong.

Because the opening action scene of agents chasing Trinity is not happening *to* Neo the protagonist. Like most prologues, the opener of The Matrix is *about* the protagonist but *without* the protagonist.

Remember, the Inciting Incident must happen to the protagonist. And it must introduce the protagonist to the story's main conflict.

The real Inciting Incident of The Matrix is when the agents arrest Neo at work and take him into interrogation. They tell Neo he will be found "guilty of virtually every computer crime we have a law for" if he doesn't help them capture Morpheus. Major Problem! And it not only introduces Neo the protagonist to the story's main conflict but also establishes Neo's Precious Want of obtaining Relief from the agents and thus his freedom from the machine overlords enslaving all of humankind.

If Neo immediately has to fight Agent Smith, which he does so here on a smaller scale in the interrogation room, he will lose. They seal his mouth shut and implant a tracking bug into his stomach as proof of that much.

Because Neo lacks his Essential Need of believing in himself as The One. His reward for believing in himself as The One is that the Matrix is actually just an illusion, and once he realizes this truth he becomes The One and can manipulate the physics of the digital world.

At the Midpoint Neo is even told by the Oracle he's not The One. Though this is a trick she plays on him to help nudge him into abandoning his Precious Want for his Essential Need.

Which he eventually does and then is rewarded with both Want and Need by the end.

But maybe you prefer a big opportunity instead of a major problem for an Inciting Incident. Okay. Everyone is familiar with the movie Rocky so it makes for a perfect example.

Rocky Balboa is living his life as a bum boxer and hired muscle for the local loan shark Tony Gazzo. He's scraping by just fine but his life isn't anywhere near satisfying considering practically everyone dismisses him as a loser going nowhere fast. Even Rocky doesn't respect himself.

The movie opens with Rocky in a boxing match against Spider Rico to contrast the final fight against Apollo Creed. Two bum boxers duking it out in the dark hole of a small "arena." Rocky is out of shape and swinging wild punches. Between rounds his corner man offers advice, but Rocky ignores it. He's used to doing things on his own and that's how he likes it. Spider delivers a headbutt and Rocky flies into a rage, pummeling Spider to the mat then continuing to pummel him until the ref breaks them apart and Rocky ekes out a win. After which Rocky asks for a cigarette on his way to the locker room where he gets paid small change for the fight.

Then one day boxing promoter George Jergens offers the Italian Stallion a rare shot at the world heavy-weight boxing champion Apollo Creed, and Rocky's world is forever changed.

Now that's a big opportunity if I've ever heard one!

And it does something all Inciting Incidents do along with introducing change to the protagonist's ordinary world: it establishes the protagonist's Precious Want.

The protagonist's Precious Want is what they believe will make them happy. Rocky's Precious Want is to "go the distance" with Apollo Creed by training on his own so he can prove he's not the loser everyone thinks he is. In core element terms his Precious Want is Possession of the respect of others.

But if you immediately put Rocky in the ring with Apollo, Rocky wouldn't last more than a few rounds at most.

Because he lacks his Essential Need.

The Essential Need is what will truly make the protagonist happy. And Rocky's Essential Need is to respect himself by training properly with help and prove he's a worthy contender. In core element terms his Essential Need is Possession of self-respect.

He wants the respect of others, but he needs to respect himself.

If you don't respect yourself then you can't expect anyone else to. Which just so happens to be the moral theme of Rocky.

"But wait," you say, "that's two core elements, and you said there can be only one. You lied and now I hate your face!"

Patience, Grasshopper.

There is only one.

If you remove Rocky's Essential Need, his Precious Want alone will earn him only failure and disgrace because he cannot go the distance with Apollo by training on his own. Which is why the dominant core element becomes his Essential Need. Rocky can only go the distance with Apollo by accepting Mickey's wiser training. But Rocky must learn this, ergo why he first chases after his Precious Want before abandoning it for his Essential Need.

At the Midpoint Mickey offers to train Rocky, but Rocky refuses and throws a tantrum because he's still angry over Mickey giving his gym locker away after his terrible performance against Spider Rico. He punches the door repeatedly while screaming and shouting his frustrations about his dissatisfying life and how Apollo is going to punch his head in. These fateful words symbolize Rocky glimpsing his Essential Need as compared to his Precious Want.

This is Rocky's "Why?" moment of inner reflection played out through his temper tantrum. And this "Why?" moment occurs at every Midpoint.

After his temper tantrum, Rocky chases after Mickey, apologizes and accepts his offer for training. Thus Rocky takes his first steps toward abandoning his Precious Want of going the distance with Apollo Creed by training on his own for his Essential Need of obtaining his self-respect by accepting the wiser tutelage of Mickey as his trainer.

Without his self-respect and Mickey's mentoring Rocky would've been beaten to a bloody pulp by Apollo, would've proven all his naysayers right, and wouldn't have lasted more than a few rounds at best.

But with his self-respect earned through Mickey's mentoring Rocky becomes all heart and no quit and goes the distance like the true contender he becomes. Thus Rocky's character growth. By finally accepting Mickey's mentoring, Rocky acquires the physical and spiritual means to go the distance with Apollo. Something he sorely lacked before.

Rocky abandons his Precious Want of going the distance with Apollo by training on his own for his Essential Need of earning his self-respect through Mickey's training and is rewarded with both.

Rocky is a rags to riches story of the spirit.

Want more examples of Want vs. Need?

Sure!

Captain America: The First Avenger.

The Inciting Incident occurs when weak yet courageous Steve Rogers is drafted into the army by kind Dr. Abraham Erskine who sees something special in Steve then injects him with the super soldier serum (Big Opportunity!) which physically transforms Steve into the ultimate physical specimen. After which one of Johann Schmidt's undercover minions murders the kind doctor then steals the only remaining vial of the serum. Steve chases the minion down, then the minion swallows a poisoned capsule and dies after a "Hail Hydra."

Steve's Precious Want is now Revenge against Johann Schmidt (who is actually the Red Skull and leader of Hydra) and Hydra who intend on taking over the world with their twisted Nazi ideals.

But Steve is a *soldier* when you strip everything away, and soldiers take orders instead of giving them. And though Steve has become a perfect physical specimen, he still lacks real world combat experience.

If Steve battled Johann Schmidt (the Red Skull) immediately after he was injected with the super soldier serum, Steve would've lost the battle because he hasn't yet learned to be a true leader through real world combat experience.

Ergo Steve's Essential Need is to become a true *leader* through real world combat experience.

At first as Captain America, the other soldiers laugh at Steve and think he's a joke because he dances around and sings on stage in a goofy suit while they face the enemy on the real stage of life and death battle.

But after Steve stops being a soldier following orders and takes his first true steps toward becoming a leader at the Midpoint by taking the initiative and leaving on his own then saving a bunch of soldiers along with his best pal Bucky Barnes while risking life and limb, the other soldiers begin respecting Steve as Captain America.

Because of this Captain America is able to defeat the Red Skull . . . then Steve performs the ultimate leader sacrifice of self-sacrifice (a true leader never asks of anyone else what they would not do themselves) and crashes the Hydra plane with him in it along with the tesseract before the plane can reach the United States and kill millions of people.

Steve abandons his Precious Want of Revenge against the Red Skull without any combat experience for his Essential Need of becoming a true leader through combat experience and is rewarded with both.

Unforgiven (which just so happens to be my favorite movie).

William Munny is a notorious murderer and infamous gunfighter with a vicious temperament now turned poor pig farmer with two children and a dead wife. Will was an alcoholic in his murdering and thieving days but has since spent the past many years living in abstinence in loving memory of his wife.

The Inciting Incident occurs when the Schofield Kid shows up and offers Will a chance at a bounty on some cowboys who cut up the face of a local whore Delilah Fitzgerald. The money will provide Will's children a better life than he's been providing them as a poor pig farmer. Big Opportunity!

But Will initially turns down the Kid's offer because he hasn't touched a gun or bottle in years, then he reluctantly accepts and chases after the Kid to secure his two children a better future.

Will's Precious Want becomes Possession of the bounty to provide his two children a better life through monetary means.

But if Will had to immediately gun down the cowboys then he wouldn't have survived the gunfight.

Will's Essential Need is to make peace with his murderous past still haunting him and learn to kill for the right reasons instead of all the wrong reasons as was before.

But Will cannot make peace with his past in his current state of abstinence. He's gone from living a life of absolute indulgence to a life of absolute abstinence to ensure he doesn't revert into the cold-blooded killer he once was.

At the Midpoint, Will is beaten to within an inch of his life by Little Bill, the sheriff of Big Whiskey, for being an assassin after the bounty. Will slinks away and is taken to a barn by his pals where he slowly recovers and sits with Delilah herself. He not only sees her scarred face but the innocent woman behind those scars. During their talk he realizes the true value of the bounty (money vs. justice) and takes his first steps toward abandoning his Precious Want for his Essential Need.

It's only after Will makes peace with his past and applies the moral of "everything in moderation" that he's able to deliver proper western justice upon the cowboys who cut up Delilah Fitzgerald and obtain the bounty to secure his children a better future.

Will has gone from indulgence to abstinence to moderation and achieved true synthesis. He abandons his Precious Want (of obtaining the monetary reward of the bounty by killing for the wrong reasons) for his Essential Need (of making peace with his tortured past by delivering justice for Delilah Fitzgerald) and is rewarded with both.

Star Wars: A New Hope.

Luke Skywalker is a dreamer stuck farming with his aunt and uncle.

The Inciting Incident occurs when two droids show up with a holographic message from a pretty princess seeking help. Big Opportunity! Then the Empire kills Luke's aunt and uncle while hunting for the droids. Luke's Precious Want is now Revenge against the Empire.

But if you immediately stuck Luke in the X-wing fighter and he had to make that impossible shot which blows up the Death Star he would've missed.

Luke's Essential Need is to learn the ways of the force by trusting and believing in something he cannot see.

Which he does, trusting the force then using it to guide his "impossible" shot that blows up the Death Star.

Luke abandons his Precious Want of Revenge against the Empire for his Essential Need of Jedi training and is rewarded with both.

I could list a million more examples of Inciting Incidents, whether major problem or big opportunity, but I think you get the point.

Find the core element of your story and the story practically writes itself.

But maybe your mind is a total blank. Maybe your muse took a vacation without leaving so much as a note behind. Maybe you have absolutely no idea what you want to write, only that you want to write *something*.

Don't use your muse as an excuse not to write.

Instead, use the dice method.

Most people have some dice lying around somewhere, usually the six-sided kind from that dusty box of Monopoly you haven't played in years but never found the time to throw out. Grab one.

On a piece of paper write down numbers 1 through 6. Pick two at random and write Possession. Pick another two and write Relief. For the last two Revenge.

Now roll.

Whatever comes up is your new core element.

Go from there.

Utilizing the core element, you can write your novel starting from the beginning or starting from the end. Or both.

But what about the middle? Is it possible to write from there?

Oh yes. Definitely.

But we'll get into more on that particular tasty tidbit (and all the magnificent details of The Tragedy Twist) once we peruse the universal plot skeleton of every story ever told, the "bones" of which I will break down in detail.

So here it is, the universal plot skeleton of every story ever told: **adversity builds character**.

I know, I know, that's not exactly what you were hoping for. But those three little words are the universal truth of every story.

Without adversity there is no plot. Without adversity there is no character growth. Without adversity there is no triumph or tragedy. Without adversity there is no story!

So let's break down "adversity builds character" for both Plotter and Pantser, shall we?

BEHOLD! The *real* universal plot skeleton of every story ever told:

-ACT 1-
1. Old World Stasis
2. New World Flux

-ACT 2A-
3. Things Come Together
4. False Victory

-ACT 2B-
5. Things Fall Apart
6. False Defeat

-ACT 3-
7. False Solution
8. True Resolution

And now with brief description:

1. OLD WORLD STASIS: The protagonist's introduction in their ordinary world as established by a unique and intriguing Opening Hook, after which the Inciting Incident (whether a major problem or a big opportunity they've never dealt with before) introduces them to the story's main conflict that disrupts their ordinary world.

2. NEW WORLD FLUX: The impact of the Inciting Incident on the protagonist's ordinary world forever changed, their emotional then logical reaction and what they plan on doing about it. They may consult a Mentor for the necessary push forward before crossing a "no turning back" threshold as death stakes (physical, professional, or psychological) are established.

3. THINGS COME TOGETHER: The fish-out-of-water protagonist progresses toward resolving the story's main conflict, achieving more

successes than failures. The building of a team of allies who learn to work together toward a common goal. Somewhere in the middle is the Pinch Point, not only a reminder of the antagonist's ongoing plans (or the antagonist's introduction if they haven't been introduced already) but also a display of the protagonist's current character growth as shown by their positive reaction to the Pinch Point. "Off screen" the Betrayal Set-up is plotted into motion if one exists.

4. FALSE VICTORY: The protagonist achieves their biggest success yet toward resolving the story's main conflict though not actually resolving the conflict itself. The team of allies working together in perfect tandem and often led by the protagonist if not the Mentor. After which the protagonist is struck stunned by a surprising "twist" of new key information causing a reversal of fortune which shifts them from Reaction to Proaction from this moment forward because now the antagonist is fully aware of who the protagonist is and why they stand in their way. The death stakes if the protagonist fails (physical, professional, or psychological) are now imminent.

5. THINGS FALL APART: Everything that has worked well for the protagonist before now fails them. The team of allies they built up crumbles apart through internal dissension as external enemies close in. More failures than successes while the set-up of the Betrayal begins to take effect. This is the build-up to the Punch Point, not only a reminder of the antagonist's change of plans because of the protagonist's interference but also a display of the protagonist's regression as shown by their negative reaction to the Punch Point.

6. FALSE DEFEAT: Tools are stripped away or broken, as well as allies captured or killed, leaving the protagonist alone during their lowest point thus far. The Betrayal is paid off in full. All is lost as hope is abandoned . . . until the protagonist is struck by a thunderbolt of inspiration to continue, jolting them out from their despair as they formulate a new plan of attack against the antagonist then cross another "no turning back" threshold showing their renewed dedication.

7. FALSE SOLUTION: The protagonist gathers the necessary resources and implements their new plan of attack against the antagonist while all remaining subplots outside the protagonist are resolved before the inevitable final battle. If allies of the protagonist and

minions of the antagonist still exist then they are dealt with here.

8. TRUE RESOLUTION: The final battle. Protagonist vs. Antagonist. One-on-one. Triumph or tragedy. Victory or defeat. "There can be only one!"

But not all stories end in protagonist triumph, ergo The Tragedy Twist.

The Midpoint (False Victory) and the Climax (True Resolution) almost always parallel each other, so if your Midpoint is "happy" then your Climax is a triumph. This also defines the point between (False Defeat) as an All Is Lost or an All Is Joy because it must be the opposite of the Midpoint and the Climax.

If your story ends in triumph then your protagonist experiences a "happy" Midpoint but a tragic All Is Lost before the triumphant Climax. If your story ends in tragedy then your protagonist experiences an "unhappy" Midpoint but a triumphant All Is Joy before the tragic Climax.

Think of your story as a roller coaster of emotions traversing both peaks and valleys, the peaks triumphs and the valleys tragedies, with each peak taller and every valley lower than those previous.

Adjust accordingly.

For the moment I want you to think of yourself not as a writer but as an archeologist. You're at the dig sight and you've just discovered the skeleton of the possible missing link.

Bravo!

So you take out your archeologist tools and prepare to unearth the "skeleton" of your story by chipping away the rock and brushing away the dirt from around the "bones" through differing methods.

Pantsers enjoy discovery while Plotters enjoy detection. Pantsers diagnose while Plotters analyze. Pantsers are emotional while Plotters are logical. Pantsers search while Plotters locate.

Though Plotters and Pantsers differ in their preferred methods of attack, they represent two sides of the same musing coin.

I by my very nature am a Plotter. Though I believe every writer begins as a Pantser . . . until they discover their personal preferred method and choose left or right at that Plotter or Pantser fork in the road. I've tried Pantsing, and even wrote a novel doing so, but I found Pantsing wasn't for me. And I can already hear all of you Plotters out there groaning that the universal plot skeleton I've provided you isn't detailed enough for your particular tastes.

Good.

Because I'm not finished with you yet, my fellow Plotters, so stop your bellyaching and take a gander at the *expanded* universal plot skeleton of every story ever told for *real* Plotters:

-ACT 1-
OLD WORLD STASIS
1. Opening Hook
2. Save the Cat & Kick the Dog
3. Inciting Incident
4. Initial Reaction

NEW WORLD FLUX
5. Try/Fail Cycle 1
6. Try/Fail Cycle 2
7. Try/"Fail" Cycle 3
8. Physical Crossing

-ACT 2A-
THINGS COME TOGETHER
9. Fish Out of Water
10. Friends and Enemies and Training
11. Betrayal Set-up
12. Final Training and Advice

FALSE VICTORY
13. Big Success
14. Empty Rewards
15. Midpoint Twist
16. The Middle Riddle

-ACT 2B-
THINGS FALL APART
17. Rededication
18. Try/Fail Cycle 4
19. Betrayal Influence
20. Try/Fail Cycle 5

FALSE DEFEAT
21.   Betrayal Pay-off & All Is Lost
22. Depression, Regret, Acceptance
23. Inspiration Received
24. Spiritual Crossing

-ACT 3-
FALSE SOLUTION
25. Inspiration Given
26. Storming the Castle
27. Subplot Wrap-ups
28. Separation

TRUE RESOLUTION
29. All Is Lost . . . Again.
30. All Is Won
31.   Immediate Effects
32. Sunset of the Resolution

I will explain each of the 32 "bones" of the expanded universal plot skeleton in detail, then how best to implement them using The Master Plan.

But have no worries Pantser, I haven't forgotten you. I also provide you with relevant information for your universal plot skeleton at every stage then leave you be so you can muse to your adventurous heart's content.

Pen the Sword guides Plotters by the hand while simply pointing Pantsers in the right direction. And though I have provided suggestions for both Plotters and Pantsers at every stage of your protagonist's journey toward triumph or tragedy, I recommend both of you to read the other's sections while offering this: take what you like, discard what you don't, and then ultimately design a plot skeleton of your own choosing.

Learn. Adapt. Grow. Create.

And above all: enjoy!

So buckle up . . . 'cause here we go.

Though one thing first.

The length of described scenes is entirely up to you, the writer and creator of your story. Just because a stage or section describes a particular scene or scenes does not mean you are required to give that section or stage an entire "chapter" unto itself.

Sometimes an entire chapter is necessary to present all the information, while other times your story may only require a few paragraphs or even only a few sentences.

The length of scenes depends entirely on your particular story.

The Inciting Incident in Rocky, for example, doesn't take place until almost halfway into the movie, whereas most Inciting Incidents take place much earlier.

Your Inciting Incident might take place twenty pages into your novel, or it might happen two pages in. It may require an entire chapter unto itself, or it may only need a few paragraphs to get the job done.

This applies to every suggested scene in this entire book. You decide how long or short because you are the writer. If a particular scene only requires a few paragraphs for your particular story then don't try to force it into the length of an entire chapter. Combine several scenes into one chapter where needed. Or you may need to split one chapter into several because it writes exceedingly longer than expected.

Either is okay.

No one is going to sneak into your house at night and murder you in your sleep because your protagonist spent several chapters throughout Friends and Enemies and Training, or that they endured their Try/Fail Cycles after the Inciting Incident all in one chapter.

Long chapters do not make great chapters unless your particular story requires them. Neither do short scenes make exciting scenes unless your particular story requires them.

Chapters and scenes should only be as long or short as your story requires.

Oh, and one more thing . . .

Please do not be put off or take it literally when I refer to the protagonist or another character as "he" or "him." I'm a man, so it's just my natural inflection to use "he" or "him" as common reference to a character. I am not implying that your protagonist, or any of your other characters, must be male.

I've tried to insert "she" and "her" when the notion strikes me, though I didn't want to fill this book with constant "he/she" and "his/her" alternative gender pronoun options and clutter it with unnecessary confusion.

So take the used gender pronouns with a grain of salt.

STAGE 1 : OLD WORLD STASIS

The protagonist's introduction in their ordinary world as established by a unique and intriguing Opening Hook, after which the Inciting Incident (whether a major problem or a big opportunity they've never dealt with before) introduces them to the story's main conflict that disrupts their ordinary world.

This is the first "bone" of the universal plot skeleton. The skull to the rest of the body. Every story must begin somewhere and this is it. This stage represents your protagonist mid-action in their old world before, during and after the main conflict of the story is introduced by the Inciting Incident and changes that world forever.

Every story is divided into 3 Acts. Act 1 is the beginning. Act 2 is the middle, split in half into parts A & B because it's twice the size of the others. Act 3 is the end.

Think of it like a sandwich. Acts 1 & 3 are the two slices of bread, with Act 2 being the yummy filling.

Act 1 the set-up.

Act 2 the conflict.

Act 3 the resolution.

The Inciting Incident is either a major problem or a big opportunity. Usually the protagonist who is living a satisfying life is hit with a major problem that only worsens until they decide to act, and the protagonist who is living a dissatisfying life encounters a big opportunity that proves too good to pass up, because the protagonist's starting state and ending state are opposites to show their change through character growth. Though this is not always the case.

Please consult the *How to write your novel backwards using The Tragedy Twist* section (pg. 94) toward the end of this book for more details on how to decide which is appropriate for your particular story and protagonist.

The Inciting Incident also determines the protagonist's Precious Want. Depending on your story and protagonist, they will eventually obtain or achieve it or they won't. The "it" being the core element that is Possession of, Relief from, or Revenge for something.

For Pantsers:

Act 1 is all about the set-up. You introduce your protagonist in a unique and intriguing way through an Opening Hook while showing them in their ordinary world doing ordinary things.

Now, I don't mean "ordinary" as in boring. Nobody wants to read about your protagonist sitting bedside clipping their toenails all day. Ordinary simply means if your protagonist is a struggling boxer then show them boxing. If they're a pirate then show them pirating. If they're a billionaire businesswoman then show them closing a multi-million dollar deal. If they're a race car driver then show them racing.

Are they happy and living a satisfying life at the beginning? Or are they unhappy and living a dissatisfied life? Remember, the starting and ending state of your protagonist are usually opposite states to show protagonist change through character growth.

A happy beginning doesn't necessarily mean the protagonist's life is a perfect ray of sunshine though, it just means they are resistant to change because they are used to things the way they are. And an unhappy beginning doesn't necessarily mean everything is horrible either, it just means they long for something "more" than what they currently have.

Then along comes the Inciting Incident which introduces your protagonist to their first real awareness of the story's main conflict. A disruptor to their ordinary world be it major problem or big opportunity they've never dealt with before.

However you choose to introduce your protagonist, make your Inciting Incident unique and interesting while also introducing the characters of their everyday activities. Friends and family and rivals and everyone else they normally interact with.

The key is to do so mid-action. Show don't tell us who the protagonist is and why we should care. There are a million other novels to read so why should we choose yours?

What skills does your protagonist possess that your other characters don't? What flaws?

Give me a reason to keep reading and I will.

After you've set them up, hit them with their life-changing Inciting Incident.

Do they win it big on the lottery? Or lose it big as the bank seeks to foreclose on their house?

Are they having a new baby? Or does a loved one commit suicide?

Are they finally getting that promotion at work? Or do they get fired because of downsizing?

How do they tangle with it?

How do they initially react?

Why did you choose this particular character as your protagonist instead of another?

Whatever your Inciting Incident, it must make clear the protagonist will seek Possession of, Relief from, or Revenge for something when they finally decide to act.

Think of your core element as a new lover. Introduce it to your muse then let them fondle.

For Plotters:

1. Opening Hook

Old World Stasis begins with the Opening Hook. Obviously named because it's supposed to hook your reader in for wanting more. They're the big fish and you the hungry fisherman, the Opening Hook your delicious bait. A ton of movies—because they're visual—begin their Opening Hook with roughly 7 minutes of action, which is the standard prologue action hook of the Hollywood film industry.

You want your Opening Hook to be as interesting and unique as possible. You want it to snag your reader by the lip so you can reel them in begging for more. So make it interesting while also showing your protagonist's particular traits and skills, their talents and flaws, their ticks and quirks.

What separates them from the rest of the crowd? Why are they the protagonist instead of one of your other characters? What can they do that the others cannot?

Also, make them "best" at something. By which I mean if they're clumsy then have them falling all over the place. If they're smart then have them outsmarting everyone else in class. If they're brave then have them standing up to the bully picking on their friend even though they know they have no chance of winning the fight.

Or maybe they do but not physically. If they're sarcastic by nature then have them spew forth a string of zingers, embarrassing the bully seconds before they get punched in the nose.

However you choose to hook your audience, make sure it's both unique and interesting.

Write an intriguing Opening Hook then find the latest possible place you can start it at and cut everything before that point to better plunge your reader into the action while also providing just enough information so they're not confused about what's going on, to whom and why.

This is the first taste of the protagonist meal so make it delicious.

2. Save the Cat & Kick the Dog

After the Opening Hook comes the Save the Cat moment, a term coined by Blake Snyder in his *Save the Cat!* series of books on the plot structure of movies. It came about from his noticing that in many older movies we meet the protagonist and they sometimes literally save a cat stuck up a tree for the distressed old lady or little girl owner mewling by the wayside. Though nowadays Save the Cat is a metaphor for someone in trouble needing help to which the protagonist provides a stranger's kindness.

Save the Cat is meant to make the protagonist likable. We see them do something nice for someone they don't know out from the kindness of their heart and we can't help but say, "Hey, good job, buddy." Because we like to think we'd do it, too.

Save the Cat is followed by Kick the Dog, and they are usually two separate though related scenes. Nobody likes people who go around kicking dogs. I hate 'em. You hate 'em. We all hate dog-kickers.

But don't get the wrong idea because your protagonist is not going to literally kick a dog. Instead they *are* the dog and someone kicks them. This is meant to invoke sympathy for them. We see something bad happen to them, and usually not because of their own deserving fault, and we can't help but sympathize.

But sympathy isn't what's special here—we need empathy. So we set it up by first saving the cat and showing what a likable guy the protagonist is *and then* we Kick the Dog to invoke beyond sympathy into empathy.

If we start off with kicking the dog we might not feel as bad for them if at all. Who knows, maybe the protagonist stole then ate a live baby before the story began. We barely know the guy so who cares if someone kicks him, right?

Thus why Save the Cat comes before Kick the Dog, to establish empathy over sympathy.

3. Inciting Incident

Now that we've established some feels for the protagonist and his ordinary world while he goes about his normal business, we hit him hard and fast with the Inciting Incident. This must be a major problem or a big opportunity. And it must be something they've never dealt with before or else there is no story because they would simply resolve the issue then go on about their merry way as before.

Failing your driver's test because you forgot to signal is not an Inciting Incident. Failing your driver's test because you ran over an old lady is.

Here is where your core element comes into play. The Inciting Incident is *why* your protagonist will eventually seek Possession of, Relief from, or Revenge for something. So make it good.

Don't just poke them with a sterilized needle—stab them with a poisoned sword!

Don't just give them a raise at work—have them inheriting millions from a dying relative!

Did you set your protagonist up as living a satisfying life? Then hit them with a major problem.

Did you set your protagonist up as living a dissatisfying life? Then hit them with a big opportunity.

These are not the only two life-changing options available (a satisfied protagonist can also encounter a big opportunity just like a dissatisfied protagonist can encounter a major problem), but because of the stark contrasts they make a great beginning.

4. Initial Reaction

After the Inciting Incident occurs you need an Initial Reaction from your protagonist. Emotional first, logical second. Not just a simple *yay* or *boo-hoo* either, but something big. The familiarity of their ordinary world has been disrupted in as permanent a way as you can make it and they have no idea what to do but scream and shout or jump for joy.

For example, imagine coming home and finding your significant other in bed with your best friend. Major Problem! Do you apologize for interrupting and back out of the room while gently closing the door? Of course not! You are devastated. So you break down emotionally. You're swept away in a confusing flood of emotions you have no idea how to deal with because you've never experienced them before.

Or imagine leaving work after pulling another double shift. You trudge home in the rain to your tiny apartment, make a bologna sandwich on stale bread because you can't afford anything better, then you check the stack of overdue bills that is your mail. And find a letter informing you a distant relative has died and has left you with their fortune. Big Opportunity!

After hitting the protagonist with the Inciting Incident they must react because that's what people do.

"I can't believe this!"

"Why me?"

"What should I do now?"

People react to change on an emotional level first because people are emotional creatures. They rant and rave or jump for joy. They scream and shout while throwing things. Or cry happy tears while hugging strangers. They point accusatory fingers before turning to the mirror and questioning themselves. Or call everyone they know and tell them about their good turn of fortune.

Then they calm down, the logical part of their brain kicks in and they process their new situation. They begin figuring out how to resolve the major problem because it's not going away until they do no matter how hard they try ignoring it. Or they debate accepting the big opportunity because it seems too good to pass up.

And remember this if you remember nothing else about the Old World Stasis stage of your story: Home, Work, and Play.

Show your protagonist's home life, their work life, and their life at play (social life).

We the audience need to relate to your protagonist, and showing them during these three essential phases of their life does just that. You can assemble the three into any combination you wish because that depends on your particular story, though each must be present at least once. And one will be dominant depending on your particular story and protagonist.

Some of us value our families and home life more so than our play life with our friends and our work life with our co-workers. Others value their work life over home and play. And others value their play life over work and home.

As example you can make the setting to the Opening Hook your protagonist's home life, Save the Cat during their play life, Kick the Dog during their home life again, the Inciting Incident at their work life, the Initial Reaction during their play life again. And if they're a real drama queen extend their Initial Reaction into their Home life again as a separate scene.

You're a writer—be creative!

Just because a major problem or a big opportunity happens at work doesn't mean it stays at work. Same for Home and Play.

People aren't solitary creatures by nature. When something huge impacts our life we seek out others and share our joys and woes. Even the crusty old hermit snaps at a bumping stranger when he's having a bad day.

Home, Work, and Play.

The number and order you choose is up to you.

And don't forget the people in it. The world is a stage of many actors.

STAGE 2 : NEW WORLD FLUX

The impact of the Inciting Incident on the protagonist's ordinary world forever changed, their emotional then logical reaction and what they plan on doing about it. They may consult a Mentor for the necessary push forward before crossing a "no turning back" threshold as death stakes (physical, professional, or psychological) are established.

This stage is the protagonist's old world now influenced by the life-changing Inciting Incident, whether it's a major problem or a big opportunity.

Your protagonist feels the influence from the introduction of the main story conflict into their ordinary world now no longer ordinary. They try everything they can to resolve the problem the only way they know how. Or they second guess the big opportunity for the change it brings.

But they are ill-equipped for the job or else major problem solved and story over. Or they are reluctant to accept, maybe even suspicious or afraid of accepting such a big opportunity because it might alienate them from those they care about.

Ask a lottery winner how many people they haven't talked to in years suddenly calls them up expecting favors and you get the idea. Or ask someone who gets a D.U.I. and loses their license how many of their "friends" suddenly stop answering the phone or have more important things to do when they need a ride to work or the store.

People are resistant to change whether good or bad. We establish routine in our daily lives and tend to stick to it.

And change doesn't just affect us, it also influences those around us. Opinions are like buttholes, everybody's got one. Social media exists as proof of that much.

Which eventually leads the protagonist into making their defining decision to act in a new way of approaching things. To leave their old world behind for the new world ahead that is the journey and conflict of your story. Because the major problem isn't going away, or the big opportunity is just too good to pass up.

For Pantsers:

Your protagonist has reacted to the Inciting Incident that has disrupted their ordinary world in as permanent a way as you can make it. Now they need to figure out how best to deal with the new permanent

24

displacer of their world.

So they rely on their instincts but prove ill-equipped because this life-changing issue is something they've never dealt with before.

Do they seek out advice from friends and family? Or hide what's happened because they don't want anyone else to know? Does a Mentor figure take notice and offer them sage advice?

Are they proud or embarrassed? Sacred or excited?

Eventually they must make the decision to act, and here is where they do it.

But how? And why?

Does anyone else tag along for the ride?

And where do they go from here?

For Plotters:

5. Try/Fail Cycle 1

The most satisfying accomplishments happen in threes when it pertains to dramatic issues of conflict. If someone tries and fails twice but doesn't try again we think of them as quitters. If someone tries and fails four times we get bored and wonder that they must be stupid for not trying a different way. But if someone tries and fails twice then tries and succeeds the third time that's like Goldilocks' just-right bowl of porridge: satisfying.

Failing twice is enough to build up the tension so that we root for them as they make their third attempt then cheer when they finally succeed.

So your protagonist relies upon their natural instincts and tries to resolve their life-changing issue as they ordinarily would any issue . . . and fails because this is no ordinary issue but a life-changer.

If a major problem they may ignore it hoping it goes away or that someone else will come along and deal with it for them. But they soon learn ignoring problems only makes them worse.

If it's a big opportunity then they may ignore it because they're resistant to change. They may believe they don't deserve it and so try to pass it along to someone else they believe is more deserving. Or they may even turn it down as Rocky initially did George Jergen's offer of a title shot.

In The Matrix, during Neo's interrogation, he refuses to help the agents in capturing Morpheus and for it is punished by having his mouth sealed closed and a tracking bug implanted into his stomach.

Neo wakes up at home and questions it all as a delusion then dismisses it for a crazy dream.

Then the phone rings. It's Morpheus with words of encouragement and telling Neo to meet their car at the bridge.

Neo gets in the car and is told at gunpoint by Switch to take off his shirt. He refuses. He barely knows Trinity and knows nothing of her friends so why should he trust them? Besides, now he has a gun pointed in his face! He moves to exit the vehicle.

Until Trinity convinces him to stay.

And he's rewarded not only with proof that the tracking bug is real but also by meeting with Morpheus where he's offered two pills and a promise.

Try/Fail Cycles can be entire scenes unto themselves, or they can be all bundled up like in The Matrix. This depends entirely on your particular story.

Regardless their effort, the protagonist's first failed attempt at dealing with their new issue earns them consequences that must be dealt with.

6. Try/Fail Cycle 2

So the protagonist takes a step back and regroups. Maybe even seeks out some advice from friends or relatives then tries again with more determination. But he still sticks to his old ways of doing things and fails again because his old ways cannot resolve this new life-changing issue he's facing.

And their second failed attempt earns them more consequences that must be dealt with. Friends and loved ones may grow angry or jealous. Or they won't stop pestering the protagonist because now the life-changing issue has grown into more than just the protagonist's major problem or big opportunity.

7. Try/"Fail" Cycle 3

The definition of insanity is trying the same thing over and over while expecting different results. So your protagonist steps back again, takes a breather and this time contemplates giving up or giving in. Why bother trying if he keeps failing, right? He considers living with his new issue as a permanent displacer of his ordinary world. Maybe even for a time he tries this, but things only get more complicated as he ignores the issue instead of dealing with it.

And that's when Mentor steps in and lends a hand. Which is why the Fail of Try/"Fail" Cycle 3 is in parentheses. It's not a true failure but a step in the right direction toward success.

Your protagonist can't resolve this issue on his own no matter how hard he tries through his old way of resolving things. The proof of that much already exists with the previous two Try/Fail Cycles. He doesn't possess the proper skills—yet. For that he needs to venture into a new world where others more experienced in the ways of tackling such issues can teach him all the while shedding old flaws and bad habits while learning new virtues and appropriate skills.

So someone lends your protagonist a helping hand to guide them on their way. It can be as small as a mere suggestion of advice, or as big as offering them two pills—one red, the other blue—and a promise.

Whatever the mentor means your protagonist achieves, it provides the necessary push and influences them into making the defining decision to leave their old world of Act 1 behind for the new world of Act 2 ahead so they can learn how best to deal with their issue.

Do they seek Possession of, Relief from, or Revenge for something? By now the Precious Want must be made clear.

And what are the death stakes (physical, professional, or psychological) involved? Because there must be consequences for their failure along with the rewards for their success.

8. Physical Crossing

I call this the Physical Crossing because in most stories the protagonist quite literally physically leaves their old world of restrictions behind for the new world of possibilities ahead. But it can be a metaphorical crossing as well. Such depends on the particulars of your story and the characters involved.

The Physical Crossing is the glue that holds Act 1 and Act 2 together. After this point there is no more set-up. The ordinary world of the protagonist has been established, has been changed by the Inciting Incident, the protagonist now has their Precious Want, they have finally decided to do something about it, and here is where they take that finalizing first step toward making progress.

In the Hero's Journey this is called Crossing the First Threshold. And to do so the hero must first confront a threshold guardian representing their old world, which is meant to show the hero's dedication to their journey ahead.

But crossing the first threshold doesn't have to be some physical battle against a literal guardian blocking the protagonist's way across a bridge. It can be, but it can also be something so simple as a co-worker warning them or a loved one trying to discourage them because that is what the threshold guardian truly is: discouragement. They're meant to represent a no-turning-back point. A point of no return.

"Once you go beyond this point, things will be different from here on out."

During Try/"Fail" Cycle 3 the protagonist met with a mentor (mentors can change throughout your story and do not have to be and stay one specific character) and decided to finally do something new about their major problem or big opportunity. The key word here is "new" because everything they've tried so far has failed and failed miserably.

Here they act on that defining decision.

Gonna take that new job offer in New York after all? Then pack your bags and call a taxi because you're headed to the airport.

Someone murdered your parents while you were away at college and you haven't got a clue except for the bloody ring with the strange insignia left behind in the family dog's poop from when Sparky bit the assailant's finger off? After an internet search and a few emails to track down an expert you rush out the door intent on finding out what that insignia means and to whom the ring belongs.

Husband caught cheating with the neighbor while you were out for your morning run in preparation for the marathon next month? You send him packing with a goodbye foot to the rump then call your best friend Suzie Partygirl for a night out on the town and enter the new world of singles ready to mingle.

STAGE 3 : THINGS COME TOGETHER

The fish-out-of-water protagonist progresses toward resolving the story's main conflict, achieving more successes than failures. The building of a team of allies who learn to work together toward a common goal. Somewhere in the middle is the Pinch Point, not only a reminder of the antagonist's ongoing plans (or the antagonist's introduction if they haven't been introduced already) but also a display of the protagonist's current character growth as shown by their positive reaction to the Pinch Point. "Off screen" the Betrayal Set-up is plotted into motion if one exists.

Welcome to the new world of Act 2, which is all about death stakes. Because one of three aspects of death must be on the line for the protagonist. Physical, professional, or psychological death. If your protagonist fails to achieve their end goal then this death they will surely suffer.

But don't let the word "death" get you all glum and gloomy. Every story has stakes and so must yours.

Without risk there is no reward. Of course, all risk also comes with consequences.

The protagonist enters the new world and makes friends while also making enemies as they journey toward their goal. They receive training and are rewarded by learning new skills while shedding old flaws.

But the road is a bumpy one which causes them to trip along the way. Though their stumbles also enlighten them because every mistake exists as an opportunity for learning.

Consider this stage the protagonist's upward spiral of progress, whereas its opposite of Things Fall Apart in stage 5 is a downward spiral of misfortune.

For Pantsers:

The protagonist enters a new world which proves a stark contrast to their old world, and this new world is chock full of new characters both friends and enemies who are mirror opposites to their old world counterparts.

Here is where your protagonist wades toward the deep end of the pool so to speak. They've never been under water before and each forward step raises that glistening surface ever closer to their necks.

But what is the purpose of thrills if not for the excitement of adventure?

So they keep moving forward as the water rises around them.

This is where the detective interviews witnesses and suspects while searching for clues on his way to tracking down the perpetrator. He visits bars and tangles with ruffians, each found clue keeping him on track despite the scrapes and bruises suffered.

Have fun exploring! Because you have a whole new world awaiting your discovery.

But don't forget to have your antagonist flex his muscles and remind your protagonist no matter how much fun they're having that there's a point to all their wandering.

A pinch point, actually.

Because that is what a Pinch Point is. It's the antagonist flexing their muscles as reminder to the protagonist of the story's main conflict and the death stakes involved. Imagine the antagonist sneaking up behind your protagonist and pinching them on the rump then saying, "Hey, remember me?"

This Pinch Point is a lesser version of the later Punch Point. Here the antagonist sneaks up from behind and "pinches" the protagonist, whereas later the antagonist walks up and "punches" the protagonist in the face. But more on the latter later.

So what is your Pinch Point and how does it influence your protagonist?

Does it stop them cold? Or is it a prodding nudge reminding them not to forget why they're really here?

Maybe it plants a seed of doubt about which new allies the protagonist can trust who may later betray them.

Often the Pinch Point is one of the antagonist's minions the protagonist encounters who represents the antagonist in some lesser way. The minion is going about their duties and the protagonist hampers said plans in some small way by interfering, either accidental or intentional.

Whatever the Pinch Point, it doesn't slow your protagonist down for long. In fact, it motivates them to focus more closely on all the clues they've found so far. Because the protagonist has a "positive" reaction to the Pinch Point, whereas they have a "negative" reaction to the Punch Point.

"Positive" doesn't necessarily mean the protagonist likes or enjoys what happens during the Pinch Point, it just means they learn from it and continue making progress through character growth. Just as their "negative" reaction to the later Punch Point has them regressing from their character growth.

But remember, this Pinch Point is also a display of the protagonist's current character growth. They've been making progress, and how they react to the Pinch Point shows how much.

For Plotters:

9. Fish Out of Water

Your protagonist is now treading unfamiliar waters. They may be scared, they may be excited, but they also have no real idea of what they're doing yet.

And they need help, which is why they couldn't resolve the story's main conflict to begin with. But they don't just enter the new world of Act 2 and find that help right off the bat.

Picture a room filled with people, none of whom you know. You stop and gaze. Scan faces. Take it all in. And hesitate despite knowing you want to join the party while wearing your best dress.

So you make a slow approach. Test the feel of the room and the people in it. You're looking for someone inviting to help ease you in to the crowd, but you have only a sea of unfamiliar faces staring back at you. You bump shoulders and excuse yourself while smiling. Until you eventually muster up the courage to join in on a conversation with strangers of a subject you're at least somewhat familiar with or interested in. You delight a few with snappy retort or interesting facts while offending others with your unshared sense of humor.

That's okay. Can't please all the people all the time.

Nobody approaches the edge of a cliff then dives off without looking. To do so is risking suicide. First you approach the edge and give a little peek. Then, and depending on your character, you take the plunge or spend a few minutes convincing yourself to take the plunge.

But those waters far below look dark. Could be deep, could be shallow.

Who knows?

10. Friends and Enemies and Training

Then you encounter those familiar with the new world, people more experienced than you because they live in it. You explain yourself and they're eager to help. You share things in common and make friends.

Of course, there are also those not so eager to help anyone but themselves. People with their own selfish agendas who view you only as an obstacle that must be removed from their way. You explain yourself but they want no part of it. In fact, now they don't like you. Who do you think you are strutting in to their world and making a fuss of things anyways?

The order in which your protagonist makes friends and enemies depends on your particular story. When you make friends, their enemies view you as a new enemy by association. When you make enemies, their enemies view you as a friend by disassociation. People are complex in that way.

Maybe your protagonist enters high school for the first time wearing the shirt of their favorite musician. At lunch they eat alone . . . until others take notice and join the table because they also love the same music and hey, do you play any instruments like me? We should start a band!

Or maybe they buy the last slice of pizza from the mole-faced lunch lady and the school bully behind them doesn't like that one bit because his favorite food is pizza and now what's he gonna eat, broccoli? Yuk!

However your protagonist makes friends and enemies is up to you and your story, but they surely make them because we are not alone in this crazy world and friends and enemies exist to supply your protagonist with new traits and skills while shedding old flaws and bad habits along their journey toward obtaining Possession of, Relief from, or Revenge for something.

And after making friends and enemies, your protagonist needs to start training to become more adept at resolving their issue. Training shows character growth while also applying lessons learned. New virtues need testing as proof of their worthiness while old flaws need testing as proof of their worthlessness.

Training can be physical, such as learning how to wield a lightsaber for a later duel against the bastard who killed your father though who really *is* your father. Or mental, such as studying chemistry for the final exam that will make or break your way into college. Or social, such as learning the intricacies of high school hierarchy so you can throw that mega bash of a party and finally become the most popular kid in school to nullify pooping your pants during fifth period gym class. Or any combination of the three.

Things Come Together is often also called the Fun & Games. This is a big slice of meat (or tomato for you vegans) on your story sandwich. This is the exciting stuff of action trailers for movies. It's the wizard learning magic. The cowboy learning to ride and rodeo. The ballet dancer learning street hip-hop. The computer hacker learning kung-fu in a digital dojo.

The protagonist has fun doing it and they are good at it because that's what makes them the protagonist of your story instead of another character.

Though the road is bumpy and they stumble along the way. But that's okay because mistakes exist as opportunities for learning, and with each stumble comes a lesson learned. Experience, after all, is the best teacher.

11. Betrayal Set-up

We need a reminder of the antagonist, and this is where they flex their muscles in some way. Right in the middle of all your protagonist's learning and training fun they are hit with something that reminds them of the story's main conflict and the death stakes they are risking. Physical, professional, or psychological. There is a point to your story, after all, so let's not forget it.

This is a Pinch Point and is almost always some form of attack by one of the antagonist's minions and not the antagonist herself because she is too busy doing other things like being popular and telling other lesser beings what to do. They might not even be aware that your protagonist exists—yet. Or they view them as nothing more than one of the many other nameless peons beneath their notice.

Whatever the Pinch Point, don't forget that the protagonist's "positive" reaction is a display of their current character growth, and it motivates them into honing their focus.

If your story contains a betrayal subplot then here is where best you implement its set-up (otherwise just re-title this section as Pinch Point). The Betrayal Set-up plays out "off-screen" as in a separate scene unto itself and without the protagonist knowing.

If you're planning on stabbing someone in the back, you don't pull the knife out in front of them while telling them, do you?

Of course not!

You gain their trust and wait till their back is turned then sneak up behind them all creepy-like and quiet as a mouse before delivering the satisfying stab.

This Pinch Point and Betrayal Set-up are two separate and distinct scenes, though it's possible to weave one into the other depending on your particular story.

You might decide on a cut-away here from the main story where one of your protagonist's new though jealous friends makes a deal with the antagonist or one of her minions. That's how Cypher did it with Agent Smith in The Matrix. "Insert me back in to the matrix and I'll deliver you Morpheus." Cypher was the failed "The One" before Neo and for that he's jealous of Neo's progress.

Though you don't have to make the Betrayal Set-up an entire scene unto itself. Be creative. Be sneaky. You can drop snippets of discouraging dialogue about or to your protagonist from your betrayer-to-be throughout Act 2A. Or simply have them shoot your protagonist a few disapproving looks your protagonist shrugs off. Or something so simple as not helping the protagonist during their training when they could have, instead pretending as if they didn't notice your protagonist needed their help. Or they may even try to persuade the protagonist into the wrong way of doing things.

You can make the Betrayal Set-up as obvious or obscure as you wish. But remember, the less obvious the set-up the more distressing the pay-off. Just don't make the set-up too obscure or else the pay-off won't resonate well while also feeling forced when it plays out in full reveal later on.

Sometimes the only necessity to a good Betrayal Set-up is sprinkling in a few snide comments and derogatory glances throughout Act 2A during the protagonist's training. Other times your betrayer requires an entire scene or scenes unto themselves where they plot and scheme the protagonist's undoing or even meet with the antagonist in secret as they combine plans for later.

And sometimes having your reader know exactly who is up to what and when creates greater tension. We've all watched movies or read novels where we know things the protagonist doesn't. And we hate the backstabbing betrayer-to-be for their planned treachery all the while grinding our teeth because the protagonist remains clueless during the Betrayal Influence. Until that cringing stab in their back during the Betrayal Pay-off finally plays out later on.

Obvious or obscure, the complexity of your betrayal design is entirely up to you.

12. Final Training and Advice

Before the Big Success to come, your protagonist gets some Final Training and Advice. There's little more to teach them because their training is nearly complete, so this is usually just icing advice on top of their training cake.

In The Matrix Neo is told before visiting the Oracle for the first time, "There is no spoon." Which translates to there are no bullets as Neo proves later when he's shot dead by Agent Smith only to rise perfectly unharmed as The One.

In Star Wars: A New Hope Obi-wan explains the force while Luke trains with his lightsaber against the hovering seeker droid. After Han makes a wisecrack about his blaster gun being better than ancient weapons and hokey religion, Obi-wan puts a helmet on Luke with the blast shield down, blinding Luke, then tells him to, "Let go of your conscious self and act on instinct." Which Luke does and later implements when he uses the force to guide his shot that blasts the Death Star apart.

This advice is better known as The Third Act Solution because it is given in Act 2A then implemented toward the end of Act 3.

The Third Act Solution can be given to the protagonist at any time during Act 2A as long as it's before the False Victory of the Midpoint, though it's usually here. It's a key piece of advice necessary to defeating the antagonist, though at the time it seems as nothing so important. And though every good story contains a Third Act Solution, not all stories present it here in this way.

But when they do *oh, boy!* what a feeling we the audience experience when The Third Act Solution is set up in Act 2A then pays off in Act 3 as we reflect back on what at the time seemed like nothing more than ordinary words.

STAGE 4 : FALSE VICTORY

The protagonist achieves their biggest success yet toward resolving the story's main conflict though not actually resolving the conflict itself. The team of allies working together in perfect tandem and often led by the protagonist if not the Mentor. After which the protagonist is struck stunned by a surprising "twist" of new key information causing a reversal of fortune which shifts them from Reaction to Proaction from this moment forward because now the antagonist is fully aware of who the protagonist is and why they stand in their way. The death stakes if the protagonist fails (physical, professional, or psychological) are now imminent.

So far your protagonist has existed in a state of Reaction. And this is the last bit of Reaction they will endure. After this it's Proaction because the middle of every story is where that fundamental shift takes place from Reaction (not in control of the conflict) to Proaction (taking control of the conflict).

And its cause is the stunning revelation of the Twist after the big success of the Midpoint which causes a reversal of fortune for the protagonist. This is often why the Midpoint is also called the Midpoint Reversal.

The Twist, whatever yours may be, hits hard and cuts deeps, or it shines new light on their darkened tunnel. It impacts the protagonist in a profound way and turns everything they thought they knew upside down. Some unexpected key information finally revealed. And it flips that internal switch from Reaction to Proaction because, *"Now, it's personal."*

Please note that The Tragedy Twist comes into play during this stage, as well as the False Defeat of stage 6 and the True Resolution of stage 8. More often than not, the False Victory Midpoint is a "happy" stage for the protagonist, which is why I reference the "usual" plot design of protagonist triumph most stories follow.

But this is not always the case, as in protagonist tragedy. Again, please consult the *How to write your novel backwards using The Tragedy Twist* section (pg. 94) for further details if your particular story requires otherwise and adjust accordingly.

For Pantsers:

The Midpoint is your protagonist's reward for striving thus far to achieve their goal. They've ventured. They've fought. They've ducked and dodged. They've been chased as well as done the chasing. And they've picked themselves up every time you've knocked them down because you're a sadistic though merciful writer who has created a great protagonist that dusts off and keeps on going.

Now is the time to pay their efforts off with a big success. Reward them. They deserve it for all you've put them through.

If they have a team of allies then this is where, after that team comes together, they work in perfect tandem.

In Gladiator, Russell Crowe's Maximus the gladiator slave became Maximus the Spaniard leader of his gladiator warriors. Here they enter the coliseum and survive an impossible battle meant to end with their deaths to entertain the crowd. But because it's the Midpoint, instead of dying they work as a perfect team against all odds and not only survive but win the crowd.

Which forces Commodus the murdering usurper, who orders the Spaniard to remove his helmet and reveal himself or die, to appease the crowd by allowing—*gasp!*—Maximus and his gladiators previously condemned to death to live.

What a stunning surprise!

And what a perfect example of the protagonist and antagonist coming face to face and recognizing each other as their true rivals. Because by the Midpoint the antagonist must be fully aware of the obstacle in their way that is the protagonist and why. Someone's been interfering in their plans as reported to them by their minions and now they know exactly who and why. Though this rivalry revealed can be established beforehand, depending on your particular story, but if not before then it must happen by the Midpoint at the very latest.

Which is one of the reasons why it makes everything so personal between protagonist and antagonist. They both become fully aware of each other as their main obstacles as well that one of them needs be removed for the other to succeed.

By doing so protagonist and antagonist are now chained together so to speak and set down the path that one of them must fail for the other to succeed.

All the clues your protagonist has followed thus far leads them here to this place of blissful discovery and achievement where everything seems great.

But not all things are great in paradise. Because as they stand with their spine rigid, back proud and head held high, someone or something hits them from behind and seemingly out from nowhere in a reversal of fortune.

This unforeseen Twist needs to happen as unexpected as you can fashion it. And it needs to sink its claws in and dig deep. It stuns your protagonist . . . then has them rededicating themselves to the cause because things are more personal to them now than ever before.

But before they do they turn to gaze at themselves in the proverbial mirror and ask, "Why?"

Because the twist has just given them their first true glimpse of their Essential Need compared to their Precious Want, and for that they begin questioning the true value of their Precious Want. Maybe even suspect that they've been going about things the wrong way.

But they've grown accustomed to doing things a certain way, and change is never instant.

They need a strong reason for rededicating themselves now that the death stakes have been shoved in their face impossible to ignore. Because those worrisome death stakes aren't just a possibility anymore but an inevitability if they fail. Whether Physical, professional, or psychological . . . it's now bound to happen if your protagonist fails.

For Plotters:

13. Big Success

All of the protagonist's training and efforts must pay off. They've been striving for a goal and here they achieve a giant step in the right direction. It's not the main goal accomplished or else the story would be over, but it's a big strong step toward achieving the end, whether Possession of, Relief from, or Revenge for something.

Your protagonist leads his merry band of allies as they work together to overcome a major obstacle as a perfect team. Three cheers hooray!

And after their big success your protagonist and allies must celebrate. Things are coming up roses and it can only continue up from here, right?

14. Empty Rewards

Wrong.

Because something doesn't feel right. That cold beer they cracked open just doesn't taste the same, doesn't go down as smooth as it should, doesn't quite hit the spot.

It's like that feeling you get when you know someone is standing close behind you, only when you turn around there's nobody there.

Or the feeling of standing in the checkout line at your grocery store and as you wait for the tally you know there's something you forgot to buy but you can't quite place your finger on it.

Or you're on your way to work but you just can't shake the feeling that you might have left something on though you can't imagine what.

The coffee pot?

The bathroom light?

Who knows.

But you're sure it was something, only you can't pin it down.

Like running your fingers through a spider's web. You can see what you're doing but the action is too vague for feel.

So you shrug it off and try to enjoy yourself. But you just can't relax because your mind won't stop toiling away for that one nagging thing if only you could think of it.

Oh well, maybe another beer will help.

It's a party, right?

And we've just accomplished out biggest success yet.

Who wants a high-five!

15. Midpoint Twist

Then comes the sucker punch of the Midpoint Twist. Everything the protagonist thought they knew is blown apart with new key information causing a reversal of fortune. Darn it, just when everything was going according to plan BAM! POW! right in the kisser.

To the moon, Alice!

The Midpoint Twist is a new and major revelation akin to the life-changing Inciting Incident that shook the protagonist's ordinary world apart in Act 1. Think of it as a second inciting incident. Only now it's a revelation that shakes the foundations of their new world. And it must cause a reversal of fortune.

Picture Neo in the movie The Matrix. He's visiting the Oracle and thinking everything is hunky-dory when out from nowhere she tells him BAM!, "You're not the One." Then POW!, "And one of you is going to die. Which one is up to you."

She's talking about him and Morpheus. Or rather him *or* Morpheus. And the choice is his. Then she gives Neo a cookie and sends him on his way.

Or imagine Luke and Han and Obi-wan on their way to delivering the droids to Alderaan . . . only to find Alderaan has been blown up by the Death Star. Twist!

16. The Middle Riddle

Ahh, the beautiful Middle Riddle.

I'm about to drop some writerly knowledge on you so pay attention. This may very well be the most important advice you will ever read in any book on writing ever.

Yeah, I said it.

Whether Plotter or Pantser, if you take away nothing else from this book then at least remember this choice bit of knowledge.

Right smack in the middle of your novel exists the main tent pole of your story. It happens immediately after the Midpoint Twist but before the Rededication. During your protagonist's emotional reaction to the stunning surprise of the Midpoint Twist, they endure what I call The Middle Riddle.

It's not usually an entire chapter but a single scene . . . which makes it all the more powerful.

They react emotionally to the stunning surprise of the Midpoint Twist, then comes the hot beefy injection of The Middle Riddle stabbing right into their spine.

Up till now your protagonist has been focused on one thing and one thing only: their Precious Want as was established by the Inciting Incident. Possession of, Relief from, or Revenge for something. It's what motivated them to keep going instead of turning round and rushing back home to wallow in the depressing misery of their ordinary world. It's why they made their decision to act after their meeting with a mentor before the Physical Crossing. Their decision thereafter is where they decided to pursue their Precious Want and convinced them by their mentor figure, whomever they may be, that it's worth pursuing after all.

After the Big Success and Empty Rewards, the Midpoint Twist hits the protagonist like an unforeseen punch in the guts and it hits them hard. Then emotions kick in because humans are emotional creatures. After which the logical part of their brain seeks control because such is human nature.

The Midpoint Twist allows them their first true glimpse of their Essential Need. And so they are now for the first time in your story going to question whether their Precious Want is as important as their Essential Need, or is even possible to obtain or achieve without it during The Middle Riddle.

As stated earlier with Rocky, Mickey comes offering training but Rocky refuses him. Rocky throws a tantrum, screams and pounds things. So far he's been training on his own, and he even shouts that Apollo is going to smash his head in. Subconsciously Rocky always knew he could never go the distance with Apollo by training on his own. Now he's at war inside because doing things on his own is all he's ever known. Consciously, during The Middle Riddle, Rocky finally admits that he can't do it on his own. He doesn't come right out and say, "I can't go the distance with Apollo without your training, Mickey!" but he might as well.

The Middle Riddle is a moment of inner reflection. It lasts but minutes, or perhaps even seconds, but it's the first time your protagonist truly questions themselves, questions all that they've done so far, questions their methods, and questions all that they're willing to do. And it can be summed up in one little word containing a whole planet's worth of gravity: "Why?"

The Middle Riddle is not a full-blown epiphany but the undeniable planting of doubt's seed as to the protagonist's Precious Want.

They don't just straighten after that sucker-punch in the guts Midpoint Twist and say, "Hey, now I get it!" then switch their tactics from Reaction to Proaction as a changed person because people don't work that way and change is a process. But the seed of doubt has been planted that maybe, just maybe, their Precious Want is not so precious after all, that it's not as important as their Essential Need, and that they cannot obtain their Precious Want without their Essential Need.

They may not be able to define with words what their Essential Need even is yet, and usually can't. But it's there like an itch they can't scratch, and it's not going anywhere. In fact, it's about to spread like poison ivy.

The movie Thor is a shining example. At the Midpoint Thor, having been banished to earth for being an arrogant and unworthy successor to Odin as king, finally gets to his lost hammer. He grabs it . . . but cannot lift it.

What a stunning surprise!

And his physical inability to lift his own hammer allows Thor his first true glimpse of his Essential Need compared to his Precious Want through the realization that his strength alone does not make Thor worthy to wield his hammer. Thor's Precious Want is to become king, but his Essential Need is to learn humility and compassion.

Remember all those corny sports movies from the 90's about a former athlete star now down on his luck and forced in some way to coach a team of seemingly incapable misfits? I could list a million of them but The Mighty Ducks is a prime example.

Guy just wants to do his job and pay off his bookie or prove his questionable worth to his billionaire dictator boss or whatever, and he doesn't care if his team of miserable misfits he's stuck with actually wins any games let alone the championship because a paycheck is a paycheck and he's got bills to pay and it's not him losing anyways, right?

But then the team comes together during Act 2A and, defying the odds of their inept athletic skills and their uncaring coach, actually starts winning games so hey, I guess this coaching job ain't so bad after all.

At the midpoint they achieve the False Victory of a big success and actually make it into the play-offs. Who'd have thunk it, right? These little bastards really do have a chance of winning. It's a long shot—the longest—but it exists.

Then the coach is hit with the Midpoint Twist because as the writer you try everything you can to knock them down then kick them in the ribs.

"You've actually turned the team around, Coach. So how about you abandon these losers and start coaching a real team of winners?"

Or, "You've done a great job, Coach. But I'm the boss and my team needs to win and now your misfits stand a chance of mucking that up. You like having and keeping your real job, right? I think you catch my drift. Lose or you're fired."

You see, the coach just wants to pay off his bookie or prove something to his boss so he can keep his job and forget about this whole coaching nonsense. Coaching the team was merely the means to an end. So far he's been thinking of himself because that's what is most important to him.

Himself.

Until the Midpoint Twist plants the seed of doubt.

Until The Middle Riddle forces the coach to question what's more important: the means *or* the end.

The coach or the players.

One bitter man who already had his shot in life or a whole team of misunderstood children with their futures wide open.

Because hey, I'm actually starting to like these little bastards. In fact, I'm actually starting to care about them. No, not just care for them but what is best for them.

Precious Want vs. Essential Need.

I'll repeat that.

PRECIOUS WANT VS. ESSENTIAL NEED.

You see, the coach Needs to be a better person and start putting others before himself. But he Wants to put himself first. Ergo the inner conflict.

At this point the protagonist believes they can have both—Want *and* Need—and it's that belief which begins their downward spiral of Things Fall Apart. It's also the point which determines if your story ultimately ends in triumph or tragedy, because there are several possibilities from here on out.

Most often the protagonist abandons their Precious Want for their Essential Need then eventually ends up rewarded with both in a new way they never expected. Though remember, "abandon" doesn't necessarily mean they instantly throw away their Precious Want like a torn pair of dirty underwear.

They're grown used to it, have had several successes and made good progress while wearing it, and because of that bond it will require several layers of stripping before their Precious Want is removed to make room for their Essential Need. Change is never an instant process, especially so when a life-changing Inciting Incident causes you to shoulder the burden of obtaining or achieving the Precious Want you assume will make you happy.

And you know what they say about ass . . . u . . . me.

Though sometimes the protagonist abandons their Precious Want for their Essential Need and are rewarded with the revelation that their Precious Want ain't so precious anymore and they end up even more satisfied with having their Essential Need alone.

Ask a former smoker how hard it was for them to stop smoking, or how many times it took them before they finally kicked the habit for good, and you'll get the idea. They didn't just toss the rest of their cigarettes away and never smoked again, more than likely they slowly weaned themselves off the addictive nicotine. Believe me I know, I myself am a former smoker.

And less often the protagonist clings to their Precious Want at the detriment of their Essential Need and they either end up with neither one or they sit there with their Precious-turned-Worthless Want only now they don't want it anymore because it has lost all its value.

These options provide four possible outcomes:

1. The protagonist abandons their Precious Want for their Essential Need and are eventually rewarded with both in an unexpected way.

2. The protagonist abandons their Precious Want for their Essential Need and are eventually rewarded with an even more satisfying Essential Need alone in an unexpected way.

3. The protagonist clings to their Precious Want at the detriment of their Essential Need and are punished with a Worthless Want alone in an unexpected way.

4. The protagonist clings to their Precious Want at the detriment of their Essential Need and are punished by having both stripped away in an unexpected way.

Do they eventually abandon their Precious Want for their Essential Need and end up rewarded with both, or their Essential Need only? If so then your story ends in protagonist triumph.

Or do they cling to their Precious Want at the detriment of their Essential Need and end up punished with neither, or their new Worthless Want only? If so then your story ends in protagonist tragedy.

For now they will cling to their Precious Want regardless their Essential Need like a buoy in a storm-tossed sea while rededicating themselves to the cause with the belief that they can have both. Because they don't yet fully understand their Precious Want is impossible to obtain or achieve without their Essential Need, nor that the way they've been going about gaining their Precious Want is actually the wrong way of doing things. Or even that their Precious Want might not actually be what they really want.

Which is why begins their downward spiral into their lowest point yet, the All Is Lost of their False Defeat.

In The Matrix, Neo has developed his physical capabilities throughout his upward spiral of progress during stage 3 of Things Come Together. But what he truly requires to become The One is belief, which is not a physical skill. At the Midpoint he's hit with a stunning revelation from the Oracle and glimpses his Essential Need as compared to his Precious Want, then begins his downward spiral of misfortune because he still clings to his Precious Want. It's only after most of his allies are killed by Cypher the betrayer and Morpheus is captured by the agents does Neo finally realize his Precious Want is nothing compared to his Essential Need.

Rocky is a shining example of the opposite proving true. Rocky first went about his training alone after accepting George Jergen's offer of a title shot, which makes his Things Come Together a downward spiral of misfortune instead of the usual upward spiral of progress. At the Midpoint Rocky glimpses his Essential Need and takes his first steps toward abandoning his old way of doing things (training alone) by accepting Mickey's wiser tutelage. Thus begins Rocky's upward spiral of progress as he strips away his Precious Want for his Essential Need.

But the change is not immediate, so he struggles to adhere to Mickey's advice as old flaws and habits die to make room for new virtues and skills.

For Rocky, his Things Come Together upward spiral of progress and his Things Fall Apart downward spiral of misfortune are switched.

Note, however, that the protagonist still makes progress during their downward spiral of misfortune. It just means they are going about the wrong way of doing things.

STAGE 5 : THINGS FALL APART

Everything that has worked well for the protagonist before now fails them. The team of allies they built up crumbles apart through internal dissension as external enemies close in. More failures than successes while the set-up of the Betrayal begins to take effect. This is the build-up to the Punch Point, not only a reminder of the antagonist's change of plans because of the protagonist's interference but also a display of the protagonist's regression as shown by their negative reaction to the Punch Point.

From here on in it's Proaction for your protagonist. They rededicate themselves to the cause with a fiery passion because, *"Now, it's personal."*

But now the bad guys are closing in like hungry wolves round an injured fawn because the antagonist is fully aware of the protagonist obstacle in their way and why. That annoying thorn in their side that's been hampering all their precious plans. The bug in the ear that won't quit buzzing.

And they intend to squash that bug.

But your protagonist doesn't plan on just sitting there until the antagonist godhand squashes them flat. No, sir. They intend on doing some squashing of their own.

But because the antagonist is now fully aware of your protagonist, everything they do from here on comes at a price.

Remember the previous Try/Fail Cycles in Act 1? The protagonist was stuck in their old way of doing things and for that they suffered.

They endured more Try/Fail Cycles in Act 2A by making Friends and Enemies and through Training, though they achieved more successes than failures there while also learning valuable lessons.

Here they endure more Try/Fail Cycles and earn more failures than successes because now they're stuck into a new "old way" of doing things.

Consider this stage the protagonist's downward spiral of misfortune, whereas its opposite of Things Come Together in stage 3 is an upward spiral of progress (though these, too, can be reversed, depending on your particular story).

For Pantsers:

The hunted now becomes the hunter. Such is the Reaction (not in control of the conflict) to Proaction (taking control of the conflict) switch that's been flipped by the Midpoint Twist and its reversal of fortune.

The detective assumed she's found the perpetrator only to discover—it's the wrong guy! All those lovely clues she's been following . . . were actually planted by the antagonist! Not only that but herself or a loved one is now the next target!

So they rededicate themselves to the cause because now it's more personal than ever brought to you by the Midpoint Twist.

They take action, but every step forward earns them two steps back. New clues lead to nowhere or down dark alleys where await them forces of the antagonist hiding in the shadows. Tools break down. Allies question the protagonist's motives or stop believing in them.

Every success achieved earns them a more daunting failure.

This is the downward spiral leading your protagonist toward their lowest point yet in the story. They continue gaining ground but at a cost. Two steps back for every step forward in their dance with the antagonistic forces.

If they are part of a team of allies then how does the inevitable inner conflict arise? Do their loyal and trustworthy friends voice their doubts directly to the protagonist? Or behind their back?

How goes the internal dissention? And who is behind it? How does the Betrayer's secretive plans hamper the protagonist's progress? Does the protagonist realize someone they've trusted now plots against them? Or do they excuse their failings as bad luck?

All those skills and tools they've acquired and put to good use during Act 2A don't seem to be doing the same great job anymore. Why?

For Plotters:

17. Rededication

Out from The Middle Riddle your protagonist eventually decides what to do next. They've been hit hard by the Midpoint Twist and its reversal of fortune. Had the death stakes shoved in their faces. They've looked in the proverbial mirror and asked, "Why?"

Everything so far has been leading up to this defining moment. Your protagonist gets their first true glimpse of their Essential Need in comparison to their Precious Want . . . and for now they decide they desire both.

"I'll have my cake and eat it too, please and thank you very much."

But they can't have both . . . a lesson hard learned soon enough.

Go ahead and try it. Buy a cake then eat it and see if it's still there when you're done, you pig.

Surprise: it's gone!

Did you really expect anything less?

Of course not. But at this stage your protagonist does. The Midpoint Twist has planted the seed of doubt, and during The Middle Riddle they notice it for the first time. That seed has taken root but has yet to grow. So they not only believe they can have both Want and Need but strive to achieve it.

18. Try/Fail Cycle 4

And thus begins the protagonist's downward spiral.

Two steps back for every one step forward. A dance with two left feet. More failures than successes here. They continue gaining ground but at a cost.

That happy team of cooperative allies they built up begins to break down through internal dissension. Some believe or even say outright that your protagonist is going about things all the wrong way. But he has excuses ready and at least for now his allies accept them. Is it all just a run of bad luck? Perhaps. They want to still believe in him . . . but for how long? Patience wears thin under the tread of many feet.

All the tools your protagonist has amassed so far don't seem to be working quite like they used to as was in Act 2A, and that's because Act 2A and Act 2B are opposites.

The upward spiral of progress vs. the downward spiral of misfortune (or vice versa as in Rocky's case).

Think of it like a mountain. In Act 2A the protagonist climbs up one side determined to reach that Midpoint peak. When he does—Twist!—someone shoves him from behind and he goes tumbling down the other side of Act 2B.

Every step they make toward achieving their end goal does take them forward but also sinks them deeper in the mud. And all because they didn't choose their Essential Need over their Precious Want.

19. Betrayal Influence

Internal dissension as the protagonist's team breaks down from within while external enemies close in. The Betrayer's scheming begins influencing the protagonist's attempts at success though as of yet the protagonist doesn't know the who or the why of it, only that something's "wrong" and "doesn't feel right" as attempts at progress fail them.

They may excuse it for bad luck as they stumble blindly unaware of the Betrayer lurking behind them and stepping on their heels, hindering their progress while causing problems from the shadows.

There may also be another "off screen" scene or scenes here with the Betrayer meeting with the antagonist or representatives of the antagonist for further scheming, or just to ensure their plans are going as intended.

20. Try/Fail Cycle 5

The protagonist is closer to the bottom and closing in on the antagonist.

But they're not ready.

Yet the antagonist is ready for them, has been planning so, and their forces are always one step ahead of the protagonist in their cat-and-mouse game.

Determination keeps your protagonist going despite their suspicious "bad luck." They get knocked down but not out. Get up, dust off and try again. Because they're not quitters.

But their loyal allies aren't so loyal anymore. Now they voice their concerns over what seems to them the protagonist's wrong way of doing things. They may accuse the protagonist of being selfish or stubborn. Some allies may even reject them outright now that things have taken several turns for the worse.

STAGE 6 : FALSE DEFEAT

Tools are stripped away or broken, as well as allies captured or killed, leaving the protagonist alone during their lowest point thus far. The Betrayal is paid off in full. All is lost as hope is abandoned . . . until the protagonist is struck by a thunderbolt of inspiration to continue, jolting them out from their despair as they formulate a new plan of attack against the antagonist then cross another "no turning back" threshold showing their renewed dedication.

This is the lowest point for the protagonist in your story so far. The bottom of the barrel. Just when they thought things couldn't get any worse—they do. Everything they've tried has backfired and now they don't know what to do. It's not bad luck anymore but purposeful strife.

Then you, the sadistic writer that you are, hit the protagonist with the Punch Point, a stronger version of the earlier Pinch Point. Where before the antagonist snuck up from behind and pinched the protagonist on the rump, now the antagonist walks up to your protagonist and punches them right in the face then runs away laughing. BAM! And there's nothing the protagonist can do about it because they've been knocked on their butt and are clutching a broken nose.

The Punch Point is a stronger version of the earlier Pinch Point. It's a show of the antagonist flexing their muscles in reminder of the story's main conflict as well as a display of the antagonist's current progress.

It is also a display of the protagonist's temporary regression because they have a "negative" reaction to the Punch Point. This is a major backslide in the wrong direction.

And now they know the Betrayer through full reveal.

Allies are captured or killed, the protagonist loses someone or something precious, and they are left alone to wallow in the misery of their darkest despair so far.

"I give up," they may say. What's the point of going on now that everything has failed them and those they trusted betrayed or don't believe in them anymore?

So they mope around.

Maybe even return to their depressing old world believing they deserve their misery and accept it as their new horrible stasis of life.

Until inspiration strikes them in a thunderbolt of epiphany and they proclaim, "I must go on!"

They formulate a new plan of attack, one last try against the antagonist and their remaining forces because the protagonist cannot accept life as is.

Please note that The Tragedy Twist comes into play during this stage, as well as the False Victory of stage 4 and the True Resolution of stage 8. More often than not, the False Defeat is an "unhappy" All Is Lost stage for the protagonist, which is why I referencc the "usual" plot design of protagonist triumph most stories follow.

But this is not always the case, as in protagonist tragedy. Again, please consult the *How to write your novel backwards using The Tragedy Twist* section (pg. 94) for further details if your particular story requires otherwise and adjust accordingly.

For Pantsers:

Those allies who stopped believing in them now want nothing to do with your stubborn protagonist altogether. And why should they? Everything has fallen apart and it's all their fault.

Those useful tools? Yup, they're broken and useless.

Your protagonist was previously caught within the dizzying tailspin of a downward spiral . . . which now ends here in a resounding *splat!* with their biggest failure and their lowest point in the story so far.

"Oh god, can it get any worse?"

You betcha.

Everything of meaning is stripped away from them. Tools. Friends. Lovers. Faith.

Then the worst happens: someone or something precious to the protagonist is taken or dies.

Blake Snyder calls this moment "the whiff of death" because here (typically round the 75% mark of most movies) is where someone is killed, and most usually someone precious to the protagonist. Though they can also be captured. Or both, as in the case of The Matrix. Morpheus is captured while Cyhper kills most of Neo's remaining allies before Cypher himself is killed.

"I give up," the protagonist says.

And they wallow in their misery like a pig in mud.

But for the epiphany of inspiration which eventually strikes them seemingly out from nowhere and they shout, "I must go on!"

And so they do, with a new plan of attack. But they need to leave this depressing stasis of misery behind in another threshold crossing before they gather the necessary resources for their suicidal plan.

For Plotters:

21. Betrayal Pay-off & All Is Lost

Or the antagonist's False Victory.

This is the Punch Point. It's a one-two combo right to the protagonist's face, then a giant kick in their ribs when they're on the ground bleeding.

An All Is Lost isn't just a tragic event but the worst possible thing imaginable, so make it good.

Just when things seem like they can't get any worse BAM! the Betrayer stabs your protagonist in the back with their planned treachery in full reveal.

"Really? Seriously? I thought you were on my side!"

When you knock someone down you don't allow them to stand back up before kicking them in the ribs. You do it at their weakest moment so you can get away with it.

And piled atop the treachery revealed comes the Punch Point where the antagonist scores a big victory. It now seems as if the antagonist is only a few steps shy from winning.

During the All Is Lost the protagonist is punished for their selfishness of trying to obtain both Precious Want and Essential Need in one of two ways. Either by having both Want and Need stripped away, or by them desperately clinging to their Want at the detriment of their Essential Need only to realize the bitter truth that they don't actually want it anymore because it's now meaningless and unfulfilling.

With the first it now seems as if both desires are forever out from reach.

With the second they have what they Want but it proves unsatisfying.

Boo-hoo, but you did this to yourself because either you couldn't make up your mind which of the two was more important or you stupidly chose Want over Need like a selfish bastard, you fool! Instead of having your cake and eating it too now you don't have any cake to eat. Or they have their cake but it's full of maggots. Take that!

This is also the place where, as Blake Snyder put it, "Someone or something dies" because around the 75% mark of most movies someone precious to the protagonist is killed by the antagonist or their forces. Though they can be captured instead of killed, like Mary Jane in Sam Raimi's Spider-Man or Morpheus in The Matrix.

If someone precious to the protagonist is captured—usually the love interest or less usual the mentor—then the False Solution coming next is all about the rescue of said captive. Which makes it the *False* Solution because rescuing said captive doesn't defeat the antagonist. But it does get the protagonist one giant step closer to confronting the antagonist one-on-one as only the protagonist can.

Often this is the final stage before the protagonist *becomes* the Mentor himself. They need this final push, they then become the Mentor during the False Solution, then during the True Resolution they *surpass* the Mentor. Remember, the Mentor was once the protagonist of another or previous story. They had to get their wisdom from somewhere before passing it along to your protagonist.

Sometimes this is a double-whammy of the mentor's death and the love interest's capture, leaving the protagonist all alone.

In classic Hero's Journey stories this is where the protagonist's mentor dies, usually sacrificing himself to save the protagonist or to hold off the antagonist and/or their forces while the protagonist escapes death by the skin of their teeth.

I call this sacrificial act the *Rescue From Without* because the protagonist is rescued by a means usually not of himself but by another because thus far their character growth is incomplete. It's a reflection of what happens later during the All Is Lost . . . Again! during the True Resolution when, while confronting the antagonist one-on-one as all protagonists must do during the final battle, the protagonist is at their absolute lowest point in the story and on the verge of total failure. But since they've achieved their necessary character growth by then they perform what I call a *Rescue From Within* and save themselves (because they have *surpassed* the mentor) while finally defeating the antagonist for good.

But back to the All Is Lost of the False Defeat.

The protagonist's life is in danger and they are moments from dying when someone, usually the mentor though can be any ally, makes the ultimate sacrifice to save the protagonist from mortal peril.

In Star Wars: A New Hope this is where Obi-wan is struck down by Darth Vader only to become "More powerful than you can possibly imagine."

In The Matrix this is Cypher at the end of his betrayal pay-off seconds from killing Neo when out of the blue Tank kills Cypher and saves Neo's life.

22. Depression, Regret, Acceptance

Having been spared, your protagonist now needs to process the consequences of his biggest failure yet and deal with their grief. Allies have been captured or killed, tools stripped away. They are alone or with the few remaining allies that also survived the debacle of the All Is Lost. Everything they built in Act 2A is now strewn rubble round their shaky feet.

The antagonist has seemingly won and there's no point in going on. "I give up," your protagonist says. "I've suffered enough and caused enough suffering. I can't do this anymore."

And they don't. At least for a time.

The length of this section depends on your particular story—as do all "bones" of the universal plot skeleton. Sometimes the protagonist spends hours or even days wallowing in their misery, though sometimes only a few moments before someone delivers them the proper encouragement of words. Regardless how long they shuffle along depressed over their total failure, it needs to happen. Nobody suffers such a horrible backslide as an All Is Lost then forges ahead without batting an eye.

They may even contemplate suicide.

Maybe even strip down, get in the tub and hold the razor blade to their wrist intent on slitting.

23. Inspiration Received

But they don't actually do the cutting.

Because at the end of their depression something magical happens, like a ghosthand reaching into their chest and giving a good squeeze on their broken heart in reminder of why they can't give up.

The unexpected blossom of a beautiful epiphany.

A light at the end of their tunnel of despair.

Words of encouragement from a best friend.

The simple memory of a loved one wafting through their thoughts.

A precious trinket such as a ring or a locket they shoved into their pocket before venturing into Act 2A they forgot about only to find it now and reminisce through fonder memories when the world wasn't such a dark dungeon of regrets.

However the inspirational epiphany comes, it strikes the protagonist like a jolting thunderbolt to the soul and recharges their drained

batteries.
"I must go on!"

24. **Spiritual Crossing**

The inspiration the protagonist receives after their lowly depression helps them decide on a new plan of attack. Thus sparking in them a spiritual awakening of sorts. One last try against the antagonist. It's crazy, it seems impossible, and it has no chance in heck of actually working . . . but they have to try.

Because it's try or die.

Because they cannot live life as is.

Their new miserable stasis proves too unbearable to accept.

If someone precious was taken captive, now the protagonist develops a plan of rescue that also brings them closer to confronting the antagonist one-on-one.

If they had both Precious Want and Essential Need stripped away, now they choose Need over Want because they realize their Essential Need has always been more important and oh what a fool they've been for not realizing that obvious truth before.

If they clung to their Precious Want only to find it's not what they want anymore, now they abandon it for a last chance effort at obtaining their Essential Need. In the end they may achieve or obtain their Essential Need, or if they're lucky they may gain both, and if not then perhaps neither, but they don't care because they have to try.

So they leave the depressing new stasis of their despair behind in a display of their renewed dedication.

This doesn't have to be a literal physical crossing, though in a lot of stories it is because the protagonist has returned to their old world in shambles and attempts to endure their new dejected stasis of a miserable and unfulfilled life until that inspirational epiphany jolts them into action.

This Spiritual Crossing is the glue that holds Act 2B and Act 3 together. This is a no turning back point.

Think of their Inspiration Received as a replay of their decision to act at the end of Act 1, this Spiritual Crossing reflecting their Physical Crossing which took them into Act 2A. Though where before they required that mentor nudge, now the grown protagonist does their own nudging because their mentor is no longer necessary.

In Spiderman: Homecoming, Spider-man is left trapped under tons of rubble as the Vulture leaves him to die. Peter wallows in his despair, and even cries. Until he's struck with new inspiration by Iron Man's Tony Stark reminding him if he needs the suit to be Spider-Man then he shouldn't be wearing it.

Inspiration Received!

Spider-Man pulls together, summons incredible strength like the true hero he is and shoves the rubble free. Renewed through his Siritual Crossing, he then takes leave after the Vulture in the Physical Crossing of a chase.

The protagonist is not only becoming the mentor but will soon surpass them into a new and superior mentor of their own.

And they need to face another threshold guardian of discouragement symbolizing their commitment to their new plan of attack, though this is usually brief considering the protagonist's steadfast determination over what's at stake.

STAGE 7 : FALSE SOLUTION

The protagonist gathers the necessary resources and implements their new plan of attack against the antagonist while all remaining subplots outside the protagonist are resolved before the inevitable final battle. If allies of the protagonist and minions of the antagonist still exist then they are dealt with here.

And so begins Act 3 as the protagonist heads down the irreversible road to triumph or tragedy. With their new plan of attack they are ready to give it one final try. It sounds impossible. It may be suicide. But they don't care. For them it's try or die and they're willing to risk it.

They've received the necessary inspiration to continue, though they may need to inspire the same willingness in others as they gather the necessary resources for their new plan of attack against the antagonist . . . then implement it.

They perform a defining action in a major display of their character growth, earning them a big success as well which proves they no longer need the mentor because they have now become the new mentor.

For Pantsers:

Act 3 should be short and sweet and to the point. Like a machinegun firing in your face.

You want everything here to hit your reader fast and hard and leave them gasping.

Your protagonist needs to "tool up" in preparation for their new plan of attack. Maybe make amends with allies if any remain and inspire in them the same do-or-die confidence that had them shouting, "I must go on!"

Though they may have to prove themselves worthy before others will believe in them again.

Then they execute their new plan of attack against the antagonist's remaining forces because one must deal with the troops before dispatching the general.

Here is where all remaining subplots outside the protagonist earn their wrap-ups, because after this it will come down to your protagonist and antagonist one-on-one.

Does someone need rescued?

If a former ally betrayed your protagonist and survived do they now get their just desserts? If so then how?

Regardless the means, the end is in sight and the protagonist needs be separated from their allies just like the antagonist is separated from their remaining forces (usually through elimination) so the necessary climatic final battle between protagonist and antagonist can take place.

For Plotters:

25. Inspiration Given

Your protagonist has been struck by the inspirational thunderbolt of epiphany to continue. They formulate a new plan of attack against the antagonist and have left their depression behind to implement it. But they need new tools and allies to accomplish it, so they seek them out here to rally the troops.

They don't have to seek out new tools and allies, but they must prepare themselves before implementing their new plan of attack.

They might return to the remaining allies of their crew who have lost faith and, after making amends, inspire them with a rousing speech to join in for one last try. They may even have to do something to prove themselves a worthy leader again.

They might repair broken tools or even acquire new ones.

However they do it, this preparation is a necessary step before they implement their new plan of attack because without a plan there is no attack.

26. Storming the Castle

This is the protagonist implementing their new plan of attack. In most stories this is a big action scene. Two armies smashing together upon the field of battle. If someone needs rescuing then here is the first half of that rescue mission. It's often called Storming the Castle because the protagonist and their remaining allies literally or figuratively storm the antagonist's castle or hideout.

They charge the field and take the fight to the enemy while screaming bloody murder. Though not always literally. They may prefer subterfuge and sneaking.

27. Subplot Wrap-ups

All remaining subplots outside the protagonist must be concluded before the story's main conflict is resolved, otherwise your story will not contain a satisfying conclusion and will feel like it's dragging on.

This is also where the remaining forces of the antagonist are dealt with accordingly, and usually through elimination.

If someone needs rescuing then this is the second half of the rescue mission.

The protagonist displays major progress and shows he no longer needs the mentor because he has now become the mentor.

But not all is happy-go-lucky because in taking the fight to the antagonist the protagonist also suffers loses. Allies die here or are injured and taken out of the fight along with the antagonist's remaining forces. Tools are used then thrown away after being broken.

War is hell with many casualties.

28. Separation

The protagonist must confront the antagonist one-on-one as only the protagonist can—which is what makes them the protagonist. And to do so they need separation from all remaining allies and aids to prove they are worthy of being the protagonist.

In The Matrix, after Neo and Trinity rescue Morpheus and they escape into the subway, Morpheus and Trinity use a phone to return to the real world.

Things are going great. Their departure to safety is imminent, right?

Wrong. Because just before Neo can use the phone to enact his own return along with his love interest and mentor BAM! a bullet shoots the phone into useless smithereens and he's not only stuck in the digital matrix but also alone.

But wait. He's not alone. Because Agent Smith is standing behind him.

This is a fork stabbed in the road of your story, only there exists no option for choosing which bend to take. And down that lonely road not only awaits the antagonist but also protagonist triumph or tragedy.

STAGE 8 : TRUE RESOLUTION

The final battle. Protagonist vs. Antagonist. One-on-one. Triumph or tragedy. Victory or defeat. "There can be only one!"

Everything has been leading up to this. The new mentor protagonist confronts the antagonist one-on-one as only the protagonist can and earns triumph or tragedy through victory or defeat.

'Nuff said.

Most usual the protagonist earns triumph in a display of final character growth which shows they have now surpassed the mentor.

Though please note that The Tragedy Twist comes into play during this stage, as well as the False Victory of stage 4 and the False Defeat of stage 6. More often than not, the True Resolution Climax is a "happy" stage for the protagonist, which is why I reference the "usual" plot design of protagonist triumph most stories follow.

But this is not always the case, as in protagonist tragedy. Again, please consult the *How to write your novel backwards using The Tragedy Twist* section (pg. 94) for further details if your particular story requires otherwise and adjust accordingly.

For Pantsers:

Everything in your story so far comes down to this defining stage. Moments from obtaining or achieving Possession of, Relief from, or Revenge for something. Protagonist vs. Antagonist. Triumph or tragedy. Victory or defeat.

But you don't want a simple victory or defeat. Here you want misdirection to wow your reader with that surprise twist ending you're not even sure about but are moments from creating. So you have your protagonist and antagonist dance back and forth in a deceptive mambo as to which is truly leading.

They tangle and twist. Drop to the floor and wrestle. Struggle tooth and nail.

But which one comes out the victor? How and why?

Do they get their Precious Want because they embraced their Essential Need? Or do they get their Essential Need alone because they abandoned their Precious-now-Worthless Want?

Are they punished with neither? Or do they get their Worthless Want after having their Essential Need stripped away?

Surprise is your friend so make it a good one. Something not even you saw coming before this moment that will really send your reader into a head-shaking tizzy though ultimately leave them satisfied.

Cigarette, anyone?

Then, after you've stroked them to completion, show what rewards or consequences the impact of your climax has on your characters and their world.

How does the protagonist's triumph or tragedy impact the world and everyone in it?

Does your protagonist live to fight another day? Does your antagonist survive to plot and plan further mayhem?

How does your protagonist dig deep down and in an unforeseen though logical way defeat the antagonist?

Or is there an ironic twist to your ending?

After which you close your story with a beautiful or eerie sunset leaving them fearful of or anxious for the new dawn ahead.

Your next novel perhaps?

For Plotters:

29. All Is Lost . . . Again!

You don't want your protagonist to just walk up to your antagonist and knock 'em out with one punch and end of story. Instead you want your reader on the edge of their seat and guessing who will come out on top the victor. So you have your protagonist gaining the upper hand, and it seems like their victory is imminent when BAM! the antagonist hits them with a sucker punch that sends them sprawling.

Oh no! He's going to lose after all!

No. He's not.

But you want your reader to think he is.

Hit your protagonist with their absolute lowest point yet. Think of the All Is Lost from the False Defeat and magnify it a thousand fold. Strip everything away from the protagonist, then peel off their skin and watch them squirm.

Don't just shove the death stakes (physical, professional, or psychological) in their faces, attempt to smother them with it!

You want this moment to seem seconds away from total defeat.

The odds too impossible.

The antagonist too overwhelming.

30. All Is Won

Because that is what makes this part all the more satisfying. The protagonist is down and seconds from total defeat. One more stomp and their fading hopes will be crushed to dust along with their skull.

This is the defining moment the new mentor protagonist surpasses their old mentor in a surprising yet satisfying way.

They dig deep down, perform a Rescue From Within and somehow achieve an impossible yet logical victory.

Yes!

Neo is shot dead . . . then rises as The One because the matrix is only an illusion and there are no bullets!

Luke finally trusts in and uses the force, pulls off the impossible shot and blows up the Death Star!

Rocky proves he's a worthy contender deserving respect and not only goes the distance with Apollo Creed but almost wins!

Maximus kills Commodus in front of all of Rome before reuniting with his beloved family in the afterlife!

Spider-Man doesn't just stop the Vulture but saves New York!

Of course, the protagonist may very well earn tragedy over triumph.

Leaving Las Vegas is a perfect example of a heart-tugging tragedy. Alcoholic Ben Sanderson ventures to Las Vegas determined to drink himself to death. Tragic? Yes. And by the end of the story he accomplishes just that. So it's a tragedy, right? Yes and no. Ben achieves his goal, thus gaining triumph. But it is a tragedy because Ben dies since he clings to his Precious Want at the detriment of his Essential Need. His Essential Need is to love himself and stop drinking, but his Precious Want is to drink himself to death.

Same too with the movie Logan. The "Wolverine" and former X-Man risks everything to get a bunch of innocent mutant children to the safe haven across the Canadian border. He accomplishes his goal (triumph) though at the cost of his life (tragedy) because he dies achieving his goal.

31. Immediate Effects

Every victory must be rewarded, and here you show the immediate effects of your protagonist's victory or defeat.

Maybe they celebrate their achievement. Maybe they mourn their loses. Maybe the cruel mixture of both.

Does a kingdom fall now that the tyrannical antagonist is dead? Or does the kingdom rise now that a new protagonist king is crowned?

32. Sunset of the Resolution

Everyone loves a beautiful sunset, so give your reader one to remember.

To which someone speaks a snappy one-liner.

Or your protagonist performs a simple action showing their new changed self which contains a whole novel of implications.

Or something so simple as a shared smile.

An exchange of winks.

A cheering crowd as lovers kiss.

The antagonist swearing revenge behind prison bars.

Whatever you decide, make it as short and sweet as possible.

And remember, most often the starting and ending state of the protagonist are opposite states as proof of their change through character growth.

For example, if they start scared and weak then they end brave and strong.

If they began living a dissatisfying life, now show them satisfied with all they've accomplished.

** THE MASTER PLAN

So you want to write a novel.

That's good.

And you want to write it both well and fast.

That's real good.

But you need a plan regardless whether you're a Plotter or a Pantser. And I have just the plan for you.

The Master Plan.

In this final chapter of Pen the Sword I offer final advice for both Plotters and Pantsers on how best to implement the universal plot skeleton of every story ever told, as well as suggestions for editing and a few other important subjects.

But first let's recap the universal plot skeleton of every story ever told in all its glory:

-ACT 1-

1. OLD WORLD STASIS: The protagonist's introduction in their ordinary world as established by a unique and intriguing Opening Hook, after which the Inciting Incident (whether a major problem or a big opportunity they've never dealt with before) introduces them to the story's main conflict that disrupts their ordinary world.

2. NEW WORLD FLUX: The impact of the Inciting Incident on the protagonist's ordinary world forever changed, their emotional then logical reaction and what they plan on doing about it. They may consult a Mentor for the necessary push forward before crossing a "no turning back" threshold as death stakes (physical, professional, or psychological) are established.

-ACT 2A-

3. THINGS COME TOGETHER: The fish-out-of-water protagonist progresses toward resolving the story's main conflict, achieving more successes than failures. The building of a team of allies who learn to work together toward a common goal. Somewhere in the middle is the Pinch Point, not only a reminder of the antagonist's ongoing plans (or the antagonist's introduction if they haven't been introduced already) but also a display of the protagonist's current character growth as shown by their positive reaction to the Pinch Point. "Off screen" the Betrayal

Set-up is plotted into motion if one exists.

4. FALSE VICTORY: The protagonist achieves their biggest success yet toward resolving the story's main conflict though not actually resolving the conflict itself. The team of allies working together in perfect tandem and often led by the protagonist if not the Mentor. After which the protagonist is struck stunned by a surprising "twist" of new key information causing a reversal of fortune which shifts them from Reaction to Proaction from this moment forward because now the antagonist is fully aware of who the protagonist is and why they stand in their way. The death stakes if the protagonist fails (physical, professional, or psychological) are now imminent.

-ACT 2B-

5. THINGS FALL APART: Everything that has worked well for the protagonist before now fails them. The team of allies they built up crumbles apart through internal dissension as external enemies close in. More failures than successes while the set-up of the Betrayal begins to take effect. This is the build-up to the Punch Point, not only a reminder of the antagonist's change of plans because of the protagonist's interference but also a display of the protagonist's regression as shown by their negative reaction to the Punch Point.

6. FALSE DEFEAT: Tools are stripped away or broken, as well as allies captured or killed, leaving the protagonist alone during their lowest point thus far. The Betrayal is paid off in full. All is lost as hope is abandoned . . . until the protagonist is struck by a thunderbolt of inspiration to continue, jolting them out from their despair as they formulate a new plan of attack against the antagonist then cross another 'no turning back" threshold showing their renewed dedication.

-ACT 3-

7. FALSE SOLUTION: The protagonist gathers the necessary resources and implements their new plan of attack against the antagonist while all remaining subplots outside the protagonist are resolved before the inevitable final battle. If allies of the protagonist and minions of the antagonist still exist then they are dealt with here.

---

8. TRUE RESOLUTION: The final battle. Protagonist vs. Antagonist. One-on-one. Triumph or tragedy. Victory or defeat. "There can be only one!"

-The Tragedy Twist-

The Midpoint (False Victory) and the Climax (True Resolution) almost always parallel each other, so if your Midpoint is "happy" then your Climax is a triumph. This also defines the point between (False Defeat) as an All Is Lost or an All Is Joy because it must be the opposite of the Midpoint and the Climax.

If your story ends in triumph then your protagonist experiences a "happy" Midpoint but a tragic All Is Lost before the triumphant Climax. If your story ends in tragedy then your protagonist experiences an "unhappy" Midpoint but a triumphant All Is Joy before the tragic Climax.

How to write your novel backwards using The Tragedy Twist.

This technique is very simple to utilize because your story practically plots itself.

Most stories end in protagonist triumph, which is why I mostly reference this typical plot skeleton throughout Pen the Sword, though that's not always the case. Some end in protagonist tragedy. It's about a 90/10 split because audiences prefer the "happy ending." But that doesn't mean "happy endings" are the only recipe to a great story.

I'll repeat two examples from the previous chapter:

Leaving Las Vegas is a perfect example of a heart-tugging tragedy. Alcoholic Ben Sanderson ventures to Las Vegas determined to drink himself to death. Tragic? Yes. And by the end of the story he accomplishes just that. So it's a tragedy, right?

Yes and no.

Ben achieves his goal, thus gaining his triumph. But it is a tragedy because Ben dies since he foregoes his Essential Need and clings to his Precious Want. His Essential Need is to love himself and stop drinking, but his Precious Want is to drink himself to death.

So too with the movie Logan. The "Wolverine" and former X-Man risks everything to get a bunch of innocent mutant children to the safe haven across the Canadian border. He accomplishes his goal (triumph)

66

though at the cost of his life (tragedy) because he dies achieving his goal.

So how do you write your story backwards using The Tragedy Twist?

Glad you asked.

First you decide which ending you want, triumph or tragedy.

As stated before, the Midpoint and the Climax are the same "feeling" whether happy or unhappy while being separated by their opposite. A happy Midpoint and triumphant Climax are separated by an unhappy All Is Lost. An unhappy Midpoint and tragic Climax are separated by a happy All Is Joy.

That's three parts of your story already determined just by choosing one ending.

But wait, there's more.

The protagonist starts in the opposite state from the state in which they end to serve as proof of their change through character growth. For example, if they end up strong and brave then start them out weak and cowardly.

A triumphant ending means an unhappy beginning, and a tragic ending means a happy beginning.

But wait, there's still more.

A happy beginning means your protagonist is satisfied with their ordinary world as is. Which is why you hit them with a major problem as their Inciting Incident.

An unhappy beginning means your protagonist is dissatisfied with their ordinary world as is. Which is why you hit them with a big opportunity as their Inciting Incident.

Easy peasy lemon squeezy.

Your dissatisfied protagonist encounters a Big Opportunity. They Willingly decide to act because the opportunity is too good to pass up. They eventually achieve a happy Midpoint. Suffer an All Is Lost. Then earn a Triumphant ending.

Or . . .

Your satisfied protagonist is hit with a Major Problem. They are Forced into action because the problem only worsens. They eventually endure an unhappy Midpoint. Enjoy an All Is Joy. Then suffer a Tragic ending.

1. Decide your ending, whether triumph or tragedy.

2. Which determines your Midpoint, whether False Victory or False Defeat.

3.   Which determines the stage between, whether All Is Lost or All Is Joy.

4.   Which also determines your protagonist's starting state because it is the opposite of their ending state.

5.   Which then determines the Inciting Incident, whether a Major Problem or Big Opportunity.

You now have the protagonist's starting state, the Inciting Incident, the Midpoint, the All Is Lost or All Is Joy, and the triumphant or tragic Climax. That's five parts done. Now you just fill in the gaps!

A happy beginning doesn't necessarily mean the protagonist's life is a perfect ray of sunshine though, it just means they are resistant to change because they are used to things the way they are. And an unhappy beginning doesn't necessarily mean everything is horrible either, it just means they long for something "more" than what they currently have.

Let's recap.

A Triumphant or Tragic ending that is the opposite of the protagonist's Opening Hook to show the impact of the story's main conflict on the protagonist's change of character from beginning to end. The Midpoint is the same as the Climax, which determines the All Is Lost or All Is Joy between.

So now we have two plot options available:

1.   Unhappy Opening Hook of a dissatisfied protagonist interrupted by the Big Opportunity of the Inciting Incident. After some personal debate, the protagonist chooses to act because the Big Opportunity proves too good to pass up, making Friends and Enemies while Training and progressing toward the Big Success of a False Victory Midpoint. Until a Reversal of Fortune enacted by the Midpoint "twist" leads the protagonist into the False Defeat of an All Is Lost. But an outside influence Inspires them into a new plan of attack, culminating with their Triumphant Climax.

2.   Happy Opening Hook of a satisfied protagonist disrupted by the Major Problem of the Inciting Incident. After some personal debate, the protagonist is forced to act because the Major Problem

only worsens, making Friends and Enemies while Training and progressing toward the Major Failure of a False Defeat Midpoint. Until a Reversal of Fortune enacted by the Midpoint "twist" leads the protagonist into the False Victory of an All Is Joy. But an outside influence Triggers them into a new plan of reckoning, culminating with their Tragic Climax.

-Triumphant Protagonist-

1. OLD WORLD STASIS
(Unhappy Opening Hook of a dissatisfied protagonist interrupted by the Big Opportunity of the Inciting Incident)

2. NEW WORLD FLUX
(After some personal debate, the protagonist chooses to act because the Big Opportunity proves too good to pass up)

3. THINGS COME TOGETHER
(making Friends and Enemies while Training and progressing toward)

4. FALSE VICTORY
(the Big Success of a False Victory Midpoint)

5. THINGS FALL APART
(Until a Reversal of Fortune enacted by the Midpoint "twist" leads the protagonist into)

6. FALSE DEFEAT
(the False Defeat of an All Is Lost)

7. FALSE SOLUTION
(But an outside influence Inspires them into a new plan of attack)

8. TRUE RESOLUTION
(culminating with their Triumphant Climax.)

-Tragic Protagonist-

1. OLD WORLD STASIS

(Happy Opening Hook of a satisfied protagonist disrupted by the Major Problem of the Inciting Incident)

2. NEW WORLD FLUX
(After some personal debate, the protagonist is forced to act because the Major Problem only worsens)

3. THINGS COME TOGETHER
(making Friends and Enemies while Training and progressing toward)

4. FALSE DEFEAT
(the Major Failure of a False Defeat Midpoint)

5. THINGS FALL APART
(Until a Reversal of Fortune enacted by the Midpoint "twist" leads the protagonist into)

6. FALSE VICTORY
(the False Victory of an All Is Joy)

7. FALSE SOLUTION
(But an outside influence Triggers them into a new plan of reckoning)

8. TRUE RESOLUTION
(culminating with their Tragic Climax.)

Note the False Victory and False Defeat are switched as according to their Triumphant or Tragic endings.

These are not the only two options available (one can make the further switch of the Major Problem or Big Opportunity of the Inciting Incident, depending on your particular story; for example Sylvester Stallone as Rocky Balboa lives an unsatisfied Opening Hook though is presented with the Big Opportunity of fighting for the world heavy-weight championship against Apollo Creed instead of getting hit with a Major Problem), but they are great examples used thousands of times in thousands of wonderful stories.

Patterns exist for a reason, if only to be improved upon.

And now for The Hollywood Secret.

A lot of stories new to you are not so new as you might think. Most movies, for example, are remakes of older movies. Screenwriters take the plot skeleton of an older movie, improve upon it, then rewrite it before releasing it as something "new."

Over the years this has allowed many films to become multi-million (and rarer few multi-billion) dollar blockbusters. But if you compare most remakes to the originals you will see the true genius behind the remakes.

Oceans Eleven is a prime example. The original movie starring Frank Sinatra is not a very good film. In fact, it's absolutely terrible. It's basically a bunch of drunks in suits who cut the lights then rob a few casinos. The remake of Oceans Eleven starring George Clooney, however, is a superb film in every way.

They took what worked from the original film, threw away what didn't, then improved upon what was left through the experience of releasing thousands of previous films. Hollywood has been using this process for over a hundred years for a reason, retelling the same old stories just with different actors and changes of location while updating them for the times we live in. They gauge an audience's reaction to a movie, noting what they liked and didn't like, then make changes of improvement to the remake of the same movie years later. Over and over again.

This is not to say all remakes are better than the originals, because they aren't. But that's usually due to an overzealous director trying to make a name for themselves so they muck up what's already been proven to work with their skewed "artistic vision" and so end up making a box-office bomb.

Regardless, Hollywood has a tried-and-true "film bank" of 10 genre plots (and 50 subgenre plots) they've used over and again since they first started filming. These 10 genre plots (and their 50 subgenre categories) have been tweaked and toyed with, changed and rearranged since before you watched your first movie, and they will continue to be used and improved upon long after you grow old and blame your farts on the dog. They are the "secret weapon" of every successful Hollywood screenwriter, and they are the reason why as you grow older the more movies you watch the more movies seem to feel the same . . . because they are.

I wish I could take credit for this, but one must give credit where credit is due. Blake Snyder brought this Hollywood Secret into the limelight in his *Save the Cat!* series of books on screenwriting.

Here are the 10 Hollywood genre plots (and each of their 5 category subgenres including movie examples) with brief description:

1. Monster in the House: *Monster, House, Sin*

A culpable hero is forced to save a trapped group of people from being killed by a monster he inadvertently unleashed.

(movie examples... Pure Monster: Alien; Domestic Monster: Fatal Attraction; Serial Monster: Halloween; Supernatural Monster: A Nightmare On Elm Street; Nihilist Monster: Saw).

2. Golden Fleece: *Road, Team, Prize*

A driven hero must lead a group of allies to retrieve a prized possession through a perilous journey that wasn't what the hero expected.

(movie examples... Sports Fleece: Rocky; Buddy Fleece: Finding Nemo; Epic Fleece: Raiders of the Lost Ark; Caper Fleece: Oceans Eleven; Solo Fleece: Kill Bill volumes 1 & 2).

3. Out of the Bottle: *Wish, Spell, Lesson*

A covetous hero must learn to undo a spell he wished for before it turns into a curse he can't undo.

(movie examples... Body Switch Bottle: Freaky Friday; Angel Bottle: Bruce Almighty; Thing Bottle: Jumanji; Curse Bottle: Shallow Hal; Surreal Bottle: Groundhog Day).

4. Dude With A Problem: *Innocent Hero, Sudden Event, Life or Death*

An unwitting hero must survive at all costs when he is dragged into a life or death situation he never saw coming and cannot escape.

(movie examples... Spy Problem: The Bourne Identity; Law Enforcement Problem: Die Hard; Domestic Problem: Misery; Epic Problem: Armageddon; Nature Problem: Open Water).

5. Rites of Passage: *Life Problem, Wrong Way, Acceptance*

A troubled hero's only way to overcome a spiraling life crisis is to defeat his worst enemy – himself.

(movie examples... Midlife Passage: Living Out Loud; Separation Passage: The First Wives Club; Death Passage: Ordinary People;

Addiction Passage: 28 days; Adolescent Passage: American Pie).

6. Buddy Love: *Incomplete Hero, Counterpart, Complication*
An inadequate hero must rise above an extremely difficult situation to be with a uniquely unlikely partner who is the only one capable of bringing him peace.
(movie examples... Pet Love: Free Willy; Family/Professional Love: Lethal weapon; Romantic Love: Sleepless In Seattle; Epic Love: Titanic; Forbidden Love: Beauty and the Beast).

7. Whydunit: *Detective, Secret, Dark Turn*
A single-minded hero must find the truth to a mystery so intriguing before he is swallowed by the darkness he desperately seeks to expose.
(movie examples... Political Whydunit: JFK; Fantasy Whydunit: Blade Runner; Cop Whydunit: Fargo; Personal Whydunit: Mystic River; Noir Whydunit: Brick).

8. The Fool Triumphant: *Fool, Establishment, Transmutation*
An innocent hero's only way to defeat the prejudices of a group is to change himself without losing what made him the group's target of disdain in the first place – his uniqueness.
(movie examples... Political Fool: Dave; Undercover Fool: School of Rock; Society Fool: Forrest Gump; Fool out of Water: Legally Blonde; Sex Fool: The 40-Year Old Virgin).

9. Institutionalized: *Group, Choice, Sacrifice*
An outsider's only way to save his individuality is by going against the many who wish to integrate him into their fold.
(movie examples... Military Institution: Avatar; Family Institution: The Godfather; Business Institution: Office Space; Mentor Institution: Training Day; Issue Institution: Crash).

10. Superhero: *Special Power, Nemesis, Curse*
A uniquely special hero must defeat an opponent with stronger capabilities by using the same powers that disconnect him from the people he hopes to save.
(movie examples... Real Life Superhero: Braveheart; Storybook Superhero: The Lion King; Fantasy Superhero: The Matrix; People's Superhero: Gladiator; Comic Book Superhero: The Avengers).

Want and Need.

Or Precious Want vs. Essential Need.

The Precious Want of the protagonist is what drives the action of the plot. They want something precious, a desire established by the Inciting Incident, and so strive to obtain or achieve it. Remember the core element. Possession of, Relief from, or Revenge for something. And for this the Precious Want of the protagonist becomes obvious. Think outer and logical. They may even literally state it out loud to themselves or someone else.

The Essential Need, however, is not so obvious. Think inner and emotional. On a deeper, more psychological level the protagonist needs to learn something or retrieve something she is lacking which provides them their necessary character growth, either by changing into a better person or by growing stronger as the person they are. And though they are unaware of their Essential Need at the beginning of their story, someone usually states their Essential Need outright in what seems at the time like nothing more than some off-handed comment, and often during the Old World Stasis of Act 1 with reminders throughout Act 2A sprinkled in.

The words can be direct, something like, "You lie too much," someone might say to a protagonist who needs to learn to be more honest not only with others but also themselves. Or the comment might be more subtle and perhaps comical, such as someone telling the protagonist caught in a lie, "You're so full of crap your eyes are brown."

And by story's end they either triumphantly do or tragically don't embrace their Essential Need.

The Essential Need provides the underlying moral of the story, a lesson the protagonist either learns and applies by the end or doesn't.

Most often the protagonist's Precious Want is unobtainable until they embrace their Essential Need, and then they are rewarded with both in a new and unexpected way.

Though, as stated before, this is not always the case, and such depends entirely on your particular story and your particular protagonist. There is no definite Want or Need to apply other than what you as the writer decide.

But if you make the Essential Need a strong personal conviction of yours on a sensitive subject then your passion will reflect this in your writing. Think of something you wholeheartedly believe in as a universal truth of life then apply it to your story. Controversial subjects work best.

Racism.
Molestation.
Slavery.
Infidelity.
Whatever the sensitive subject, choose a strong personal conviction then make a stand and your passion will reflect in your writing.

One sentence to rule them all!

What follows is a simple "formula" that will help guide your writing muse whether you're a Plotter or Pantser. It's not quite a Premise and it's not quite a Logline, instead it's a simple sentence designed to keep you on track with your novel. And the "formula" is simple because it's nothing more than a fill-in-the-blank.

My novel is a (*genre*) about a (*adjective + occupation*) who is (*death stakes situation*).

For example:

My novel is a *cyberpunk sci-fi* about an *anti-social computer hacker* who is *hunted by the evil robot overlords enslaving all of humanity.* – The Matrix.

My novel is a *sports-drama* about a *down-on-his-luck boxer* who is *given the rare chance to fight for the world heavy-weight championship.* –Rocky.

My novel is a *comedy* about a *pathological-lying lawyer* who is *cursed with having to tell nothing but the truth for 24 hours during the day of his biggest case.* –Liar, Liar.

My novel is a *western* about an *alcoholic former gunslinger* who is *hunted by a small-town sheriff for taking one last assassination job.* – Unforgiven.

My novel is a *romantic comedy* about a *chauvinist man and a spunky woman* who are *perfect for each other if only they can stop arguing about everything for more than five seconds.* –When Harry Met Sally.

They aren't perfect, nor do they describe in great detail their particular stories other than the overall gist of things, but they do give you an idea of what the story is about.

You can change yours, tweak it, add to or subtract from it at your leisure. And you can use yours as a reference whenever you feel lost or begin meandering into writing scenes that might have nothing to do with your overall story to help keep you on the right track.

Think of it like this. You're in New York and you wish to take a cross-country trip to California. Knowing you are driving from New York to California doesn't dictate the exact route in-between, but it does provide you with an overall plan as to how to get there: go west!

For Pantsers:

You hate plot.

I get it.

To you plot is one of the dirty four-letter words your mother used to wash your mouth out with soap for speaking.

Why would anyone want to know what happens in their novel before they even write it?

For you the joy of writing a mystery is not knowing the who dun it till you get there.

You enjoy creating wonderfully complex characters, hitting them with a major problem or a big opportunity then releasing them into the wilds of discovery while you sit back and describe what happens next because you don't know what happens next until it happens.

You're the type of person who likes cruising around on a lazy Sunday searching for yard sales while having no set course for the day but for the entertainment of wandering.

So for you I advise the following. Use the universal plot skeleton of every story ever told simply as a means of dreaming up possibilities and nothing more. No one is holding a gun to your head and making you write around specific plot points. If something strikes your fancy then use it as inspiration. If something doesn't then just ignore it.

Though I do suggest picking a desired total word count for your novel-to-be and dividing by 8. You don't have to achieve this exact word count, but this does give you a goal to work toward when you sit down and write each day.

You've made notes mental or otherwise of your story about each of the 8 main stages. Don't take them as written law but suggestions. Read them over. Think through them. Absorb them. Allow them to dance through your mind as you perceive all the wonderful possibilities of your story.

Now write.

Let your Pantsing muse guide you along while you discover your story as you write it.

If you don't like something you've already thought out ahead then change it. If you envisioned a particular scene in your head but it comes out wrong on paper then throw it away and replace it with something completely fresh.

This is *your* novel. Ultimately everything that happens in it is up to *you*. There is no paint-by-numbers formula when it comes to writing. Even Plotters don't follow an exact detailed plan because a plot skeleton isn't a strict diagram of requirements but a bountiful array of options.

Choose at your own discretion.

So close your eyes and dip your writerly brush into a random color then let the whims of your muse guide your unhindered strokes. You may not know the painting you wish to create, only that you want to paint it. So go ahead and paint by feel because that's what you're best at.

That's why you write.

For Plotters:

If I had a nickel for every time someone said they wanted to write a novel but don't have the time then I'd be a rich man. And if I had a penny for every person who started writing a novel but never actually finished it then I'd be even richer. Most people get all excited about writing their novel. They sit down and start writing—

Then the phone rings and they answer it.

Or someone knocks at their door and they see who it is.

Or their belly grumbles so they make something to eat.

Or they glance at the clock and realize their favorite show is about to start so they watch it with the intent of returning to their writing later.

Laundry? Maybe I should do that now and get it out of the way.

Dishes? They aren't going to wash themselves.

The dog wants a walk.

The cat needs a flea bath.

The kids want to play.

Or worse . . . they write a few exciting scenes after which they have absolutely no idea how to connect them or what to write next.

The #1 enemy of every writer is procrastination. Plenty of writers start novels but a lot never finish them.

Procrastination is your mortal enemy as a writer. Think of writing your novel as a story unto itself. You are its protagonist and procrastination is your antagonist. It doesn't just want you to fail but needs you to fail. It hates every day you spend writing against it. It will call your phone. It will knock on your door. It will invite you to parties and it will call your name from the television's enticing glow of screen promising your favorite shows if only you'd stop writing and enjoy the idiot box.

But you won't. Because you're a writer and you have a novel to finish. Procrastination be damned!

You will dedicate the next 40 days to writing your novel. After which you will have a complete first draft. What you do with it after that is up to you, but at least you'll have accomplished the task that defeats most wannabe writers by actually having a finished novel.

Buy a couple packs of index cards.

I want you to think about every possible scene of your novel-to-be. On each index card write a description of a single scene. These can be as simple or complex as you desire. "Car chase" or "Henry breaks into his neighbor's house and poisons their milk for calling the cops on his party" or whatever helps you remember the scenes in question. Write down as many ideas as you can come up with, even the bad ones. Particularly the bad ones so you can root them out then throw them away.

Remember, the first ideas that come to your mind while writing might reflect the first ideas that come to your reader's mind while reading, and that removes all unpredictability from your story.

If it helps, think about every fear and joy you've experienced throughout life and write them down, too. That childhood bully you never did get revenge against? Write down the worst things they ever did to you as well as all the vicious things you wanted to do in retaliation. The blissfully awkward encounter with your first lover? Write it down in all its embarrassing glory. Now is not the time to be shy, now is the time to be brutally honest. Cut open those emotional scars and let them bleed all over your index cards.

Do as many of the cards as possible. Then mix them up, shuffle them, look through them. Order then reorder them.

Now go back through this book, review each and every "bone" of the expanded universal plot skeleton of every story ever told for real Plotters then pick out 32 of your best index cards. Title and arrange them into the order of the 32 "bones" of the plot skeleton.

Now sit back and evaluate your new story skeleton.

Do the scenes move one into the other with a logical sense of flow while still containing unexpected twists? If not then change some cards around. Find ways to insert unexpected twists to surprise your potential reader. Add more cards where needed while replacing or removing others.

Once you have all 32 cards in order, stack them up then forget about them for the moment. Because I lied earlier—sort of—when I presented the universal plot skeleton of every story ever told.

What I've done is applied it to the protagonist, thusly:

-ACT 1-
1. Old World Stasis
2. New World Flux

-ACT 2A-
3. Things Come Together
4. False Victory

-ACT 2B-
5. Things Fall Apart
6. False Defeat

-ACT 3-
7. False Solution
8. True Resolution

But it also applies to the antagonist, just with a few different names and in a slightly different sequence:

-ACT 1-
1. Ordinary World
2. Driving Obsession

-ACT 2A-
3. Ongoing Action
4. Change of Plans

-ACT 2B-
5. Things Come Together
6. False Victory

-ACT 3-
7. Things Fall Apart
8. True Defeat

Note that the antagonist plot skeleton applies in accordance to the typical protagonist triumph plot skeleton.

The key difference between the protagonist and antagonist plot skeletons is simple. The protagonist eventually abandons their Precious Want for their Essential Need (unless a tragedy), whereas the antagonist clings to their Precious Want at the detriment of their Essential Need.

This key difference is what allows the protagonist to defeat the antagonist. It's what earns the protagonist their triumph while delivering the antagonist their tragedy. The consequence for the antagonist clinging to their Precious Want is defeat, while victory is the protagonist's reward for choosing their Essential Need.

But don't forget as I've stated before, even though most stories end in protagonist triumph there exist those ending in protagonist tragedy. Remember The Tragedy Twist and adjust accordingly. But let's not get off track from the norm.

The worst antagonist is a static antagonist. One who sits there twiddling their tyrannical thumbs until the protagonist shows up to confront them about their dominating plans. So don't.

Introduce the antagonist in the middle of their plans before your story begins, just as you should the protagonist. These plans are ongoing during your protagonist's Old World Stasis, only the protagonist isn't made aware of them until the Inciting Incident happens.

The antagonist isn't just after something, he's obsessed with achieving or obtaining it, whatever "it" may be. This Driving Obsession is what makes your antagonist not just any lawyer but the top shark at his firm. Not just the company president but the ruthless CEO billionaire. Not just the king of the kingdom but the tyrannical dictator of the country.

One of the main differences between the protagonist and antagonist is that while the antagonist is willing to sacrifice anything to achieve their end goal even to the detriment of those around them, the protagonist is willing to sacrifice everything to achieve their end goal though only to the detriment of themselves.

So the antagonist continues about their merry way with their own Ongoing Action as Things Come Together for your protagonist.

During the protagonist's False Victory, the antagonist suffers a Change of Plans brought about by the protagonist's interference and they are forced to finally pay attention to and eventually confront the protagonist or else the interference will only worsen.

So Things Come Together for the antagonist's new Change of Plans as Things Fall Apart for your protagonist because now the antagonist is taking aggressive steps toward removing the annoying obstacle that is the protagonist out from their way.

Until the antagonist enjoys their False Victory that is the protagonist's False Defeat.

But—Twist!—the protagonist isn't beat just yet. They're inspired with a new plan of attack then implement their False Solution, causing Things to Fall Apart for the antagonist.

Which culminates in the antagonist's True Defeat brought about by the protagonist's True Resolution because your protagonist has abandoned their Precious Want for their Essential Need while your antagonist clings to their Precious Want like grim death. And thus the universal truth of your story is proven.

It's important here to understand that the 32 "bones" are not implemented for the antagonist's plot skeleton. For this you will use a vague application of the 8 larger stages as would a Pantser. One, because the antagonist doesn't get such detail added to their story or else they would become a tragic protagonist. And Two, not all of the "bones" actually apply to the antagonist plot skeleton.

And do not apply the "acts" of the antagonist's plot skeleton as law, either. I've shown them only as example in comparison to the protagonist's plot skeleton for ease of reference. Think of them as possibilities where you can add in scenes or chapters of your antagonist's doings as according to your story. They offer breaks from the protagonist's main story goal as shown either through the antagonist's point of view or through an unfiltered perspective without the protagonist present. Use them to foreshadow events the protagonist isn't aware of because they happen "off screen" without the protagonist's knowing.

You do not have to use the 8 stages for your antagonist, nor do you need to apply them accordingly as they are titled. The antagonist plot skeleton is there for your choosing leisure to help you create a more formidable and represented antagonist obstacle instead of a boring static paper tiger.

Because every antagonist believes they are the hero of their own journey. And they view the protagonist as their antagonist obstacle in their way. If you sat them down, both could present convincing arguments as to why they should triumph over the other.

The Ordinary World of the antagonist is that of their previous ongoing plans. Striving to obtain their Driving Obsession creates or causes the protagonist's Inciting Incident, from which they have now set the protagonist on course against them for the rest of your protagonist's story.

Before this the antagonist was going about their usual business and causing Inciting Incidents to a whole slew of others. What makes your protagonist the protagonist is that when they encounter their Inciting Incident they eventually decide to do something about it whereas the others accepted the Inciting Incident's impact as a new permanent displacer of their ordinary world.

The antagonist's Ongoing Action is them implementing the next stages of their plans. But their Change of Plans arise because they can no longer ignore the protagonist interfering in said plans.

So Things Come Together for the antagonist as they seek to rid themselves of the pesky protagonist. And they achieve a False Victory, seemingly squashing the protagonist like a bug.

But the protagonist refuses to quit and so Things Fall Apart for the antagonist as the protagonist implements their new plan of attack. Then the antagonist suffers their True Defeat because, well, that's what most antagonist usually suffer when finally confronted by the protagonist in a final battle.

But not always. Consult The Tragedy Twist and adjust accordingly.

The antagonist plot skeleton is not law, nor is it required. By this point you should have many possible scenes of your antagonist you can write brought about from the actions of your protagonist striving to achieve their end goal. The antagonist plot skeleton is merely a suggestion, nothing more.

Pick 8 antagonist scenes and work them into your story to make 40 out from 32. These you will write without the filter of the protagonist's point of view, and these you can interweave into your protagonist's universal plot skeleton however you see fit.

Simple as eating cake.

Once you have all 40 index cards in order, stack them up then forget about them. Allow your mind to rest while you relax. Drink a beer and watch some television. Play with the kids. Walk the dog. Take a nap.

Enjoy it now because tomorrow the work begins.

How to math your novel.

You now have 40 index cards, each of which represents one chapter of your novel. These aren't set in stone as chapters, but the "chapter" designation will help you achieve a daily word count goal and keep you writing. Later you can combine shorter chapters or separate longer ones into several at your writing leisure. But for now let's just keep things simple.

40 cards, 40 chapters.

Choose the estimated total word count for your novel then divided by 40 to get your word count goal per chapter.

As example we'll use an 80,000 word novel because 80,000 words is the rough average of a novel. Which will give you 2,000 words per chapter.

That's writing just 2,000 measly words per day.

Now you will sit down every day for the next 40 days and write one chapter. 2,000 words. No more and no less.

Once you reach your word count goal for the day then you are done. Even if you could write more, don't. You don't want to start racing out of the gates only to slow down into an agonizing crawl halfway to the finish line. If you could write more then spend only a minute or two making some notes for future reference then stop for the day.

Pat yourself on the back. But not too much, it's only day one. Don't get cocky. 39 more to go.

Also, you do not have to begin with chapter one. In fact: don't.

Have a fantastic scene burning in your brain just waiting to get out? Then write that chapter first. So what if it's chapter seven, or chapter twenty-six, or even chapter forty. Write to your heart's desire so long as you achieve your chapter word count for the day regardless the order.

If something pops into your brain about another chapter while writing, do not switch chapters. That's just your procrastination antagonist trying to deviate you from accomplishing your goal. Instead of switching chapters just pause and jot down a few notes for later reference then go right back to finishing your chapter for the day.

40 days later and you now have a finished first draft.

Congratulations!

You've just accomplished what prevents most writers from becoming authors.

But you're not done yet because now the real work begins.

Writing is 10% writing and 90% rewriting,
and
Write first, edit last.

You've written your novel, now you need to rewrite it.

Also, edit.

Get those notes ready because for the next 40 days you will rewrite and edit your novel one chapter per day same as before, only this time you will start with chapter one and work in sequential order until finished.

Kill your darlings. If you wrote a beautiful scene that displays your writer genius in all its wonderful vainglory but it contributes nothing to your story then bite the bullet and cut it. You don't have to delete it out from existence, just from your current novel. Copy then paste it into a different file, save it for later for perhaps another novel that you'll work it into by changing the character names and setting.

Omit needless words (I cannot stress this enough). If you told us your protagonist has black hair in chapter one, we don't need reminding every time you mention her long raven flow of locks. It's black. We get it. You don't need to specify the color every time she brushes it behind an ear. And don't have people sitting "down" or standing "up" either. The direction is implied by the word. He sat. She stood. 'Nuff said.

Find "suddenly" and delete it. There are better ways to describe the indicated actions. The door suddenly slammed shut? No, the door slammed shut. It didn't take twenty minutes to slam shut, did it? Obviously not.

Shorten dialogue so everyone isn't Hello'ing and Goodbye'ing every time they encounter someone, or describing the banal minutiae of their daily routines through pointless conversation before and after the real reason for their talking. Get to the point so the conversation doesn't drag on. We don't care how Jimmy's eggs tasted at breakfast or that Tammy woke up then peed then brushed her teeth then washed her face then watered the plants then *blah blah blah* if it doesn't impact the story. And use said for most if not all of your dialogue tags. Though don't put he said/she said dialogue tags on every spoken line. Clutter distracts, and most often the dialogue itself implies who is speaking and to whom.

Don't use overlong and complicated words when shorter and simpler words will do. Nobody is impressed by your extensive vocabulary if they have to stop reading every few pages and grab a dictionary.

Seek out all –*ly* adverbs and cut them like they're going out of style. Because they did and they're never coming back.

Joe ran fastly? Barbara sighed softly? Jim shouted loudly?

No!

How can one run but fast? How can one sigh but soft? How can one shout but loud?

Exactly.

Joe ran. Barbara sighed. Jim shouted.

'Nuff said.

Remember, most of the time you see an –*ly* adverb, it and the word preceding it are better replaced with a superior single word.

Mark ran fastly?

No, Mark sprinted.

Beatrice stared meanly?

No, Beatrice glared.

And for goodness' sake make those passive sentences active!

Heather looked at her watch and saw she was going to be late if she did not hurry?

No!

Heather glanced at her watch. *Half past four already? Oh crap!* She snatched her purse from the bed and rushed for the door, bumping past Sarah without apology.

Timothy was tired?

No!

Yawning, Timothy slid his heels out and stretched both arms overhead, his heavy lids fluttering, the chair creaking beneath his strain.

Did you catch the unnecessary word in the previous sentence?

Stretched both arms.

Both.

Arms.

Both is implied by the plural of arms.

Yawning, Timothy slid his heels out and stretched his arms overhead, his heavy lids fluttering, the chair creaking beneath his strain.

Show, don't tell.

What follows is a brief checklist with before and after examples on how best to self-edit your writing so your potential publisher doesn't have to.

Omit needless words

She turned and looked behind.
She glanced back.

He gave an address to the audience.
He addressed the audience.

The police took him into custody.
The police arrested him.

She has the ability to...
She can...

Change passive voice to active voice

He was hit by the train.
The train hit him.

The football was thrown by the boy.
The boy threw the football.

Less *–ing* words

He began pacing the room.
He paced the room.

He started walking toward the door.
He walked toward the door.

The noise was coming from her left.
The noise came from her left.

Stop serving two opposing masters

Reaching for the stick, he threw it at the cat.

He picked up the stick and threw it at the cat.
He threw a stick at the cat.

Running to the car, she opened the door and dove inside.
She ran to the car, opened the door and dove inside.

Reaching for the phone, he called Tommy.
He grabbed the phone and called Tommy.
He called Tommy.

Remove character filters

He felt the car stop.
The car stopped.

Sally watched as he picked up the book.
He picked up the book.

He wondered what she meant by that.
What did she mean by that?

I want the blue one, he thought.
He wanted the blue one.
I want the blue one.

She could see his knuckles turn white.
His knuckles turned white.

Less infinitives

He began to hobble along the sidewalk.
He hobbled along the sidewalk.

The wolf's eyes seemed to glow in the moonlight.
The wolf's eyes glowed in the moonlight.

Avoid "expletive" and "had___that" constructions

There are twenty runners who have entered the race.
Twenty runners have entered the race.

She had hair that flowed past her shoulders.
Her hair flowed past her shoulders.

Shorten verbs

He would be able to get his driver's license in two months.
He could get his driver's license in two months.

Eliminate double verbs.

She reached forth and picked up the puppy.
She picked up the puppy.

He sat and watched television all day.
He watched television all day.

Eliminate double nouns, adjectives, and adverbs

"That is complete and utter nonsense."
"That's nonsense."
"Nonsense."

"The plain and simple fact is I'm not hungry."
"The fact is I'm not hungry."
"I'm not hungry."

She solved the problem wholly and completely.
She solved the problem.
Problem solved.

No wandering eyes

His eyes were glued to the computer screen.
He stared at the computer screen.

Her eyes roamed around the party.
She gazed round the party.

Delete –*ly* words

"It's none of your business," she said hotly.
"It's none of your business!"

John slowly crawled across the floor.
John crawled across the floor.

"Put that down," he said angrily.
"Put that down," he said.
"Put that down!"

Get rid of all dialogue tags except "said"

"The body wasn't there," Angie lied.
"The body wasn't there," Angie said.

"I love you," John urged.
"I love you," John said.

"Maybe some day," Patricia sighed.
"Maybe some day," Patricia said.

"I'll use my pocketknife," Steve volunteered.
"I'll use my pocketknife," Steve said.

"It was my fault," Mary admitted.
"It was my fault," Mary said.

Now get rid of "said"

"Maybe some day," Patricia said.
Patricia sighed. "Maybe some day."

"I'll use my pocketknife," Steve said.
Steve dug out his pocketknife and smirked. "This might work."

"It was my fault," Mary said.
Mary nodded, glanced away. "It was my fault."

Shorten dialogue

"Hello, Suzie. Have you seen the break room today? I just came from there on my way back to my desk and I saw a big puddle on the floor from someone spilling water then leaving it there."
"Hey Suzie, you seen the break room? What a mess. Water everywhere!"

Eliminate redundancies

The garden was overgrown with weeds that grew everywhere.
Weeds filled the garden.

"Why, good morning, Heather," Eric said in a friendly tone while smiling and waving.
Eric smiled, waved. "Good morning, Heather."

"Yesterday afternoon," was her two-word reply.
"Yesterday afternoon."

Less prepositional phrases

When they got to the bottom of the stairs...
When they reached the stair's bottom...

Sara spread a blanket on the grassy bank of the river.
Sara spread a blanket on the grassy riverbank.

Betty slapped him on the face.
Betty slapped his face.
Betty slapped him.

The floor in the basement was wet.
The basement floor was wet.
The floor was wet.

Eliminate superficials

"It goes without saying that I will be there for you."
"I'll be there for you."

"As a matter of fact, it's larger than the other one."
"It's larger than the other."

"For your information, I'm very tired."
"I'm very tired."
"I'm exhausted."

"I'd like to take this opportunity to thank you."
"Thank you."
"Thanks."

"Please be advised that it is very icy outside."
"It's icy out."

"In my opinion, it smells delicious."
"It smells delicious."

Avoid clichés

Dropping the ball.
The calm before the storm.
Crying shame.
Beat around the bush.
Tough as nails.
Crystal clear.
Hit the nail on the head.
Slept like a log.
When it rains, it pours.
All is fair in love and war.
Writing on the wall.
Last straw.
Sow one's wild oats.
Straight as an arrow.
Wise as an owl.
Sly as a fox.
Blind as a bat.
Light as a feather.
. . . you "get the picture."

Less "hads"

She had arrived late to her new job. Her boss had been angry. She had hid in her cubicle hoping he wouldn't notice, but he had.

She had arrived late to her new job. Her boss was angry. She hid in her cubicle hoping he wouldn't notice, but he did.

Omit needless words!

Ahead of them was a wrecked tractor.
Ahead was a wrecked tractor.
Wrecked tractor ahead.

He suddenly hiccupped.
He hiccupped.

Suddenly lightning flashed brightly.
Lightning flashed.

Bill sat down on the couch and opened the book then began reading.
Bill sat and read.

She knew that Jack was lying to her.
She knew Jack was lying.

The nanny brought the children toys to play with.
The nanny brought the children toys.

Whew! Another 40 days later and you now have a finished novel.

Congratulations!

I suggest waiting a week or two to let your novel "rest" before you give it a final read and apply some finishing touches.

Dive into a great book from your favorite author or work on another project.

After which, sit down with the intent of reading your novel from start to finish with as few breaks as possible.

Triple-check spelling and grammar and punctuation. Cross those i's and dot those t's. Remove unnecessary commas. Find repeated words and eliminate them.

For Both:

There is no getting around the fact that even as a Pantser you must plot, if only the tiniest amount. Why? Because certain events must happen at certain times to your protagonist in order for your story to be a coherent presentation then resolution of conflict to your reader.

You cannot have an All Is Lost of a False Defeat happen before your protagonist's decision to act made during New World Flux because that doesn't make logical sense. You cannot have the triumph or tragedy of the True Resolution happen before the major problem or big opportunity of the Inciting Incident because that doesn't make logical sense.

Your protagonist cannot deal with a life-changing issue they aren't even aware of and has yet to influence them in some way.

But this doesn't mean you are locked in to a particular way of writing, either.

And so too for Plotters.

Just because a section suggests Betrayal Pay-off after Try/Fail Cycle 5 doesn't mean you must have the betrayal happen at that particular point or else worlds will collide and existence will end. Just because a stage suggests Friends and Enemies and Training doesn't mean they must happen in said particular order or after Fish Out of Water but before the Betrayal Set-up.

Pen the Sword is a teaching guide of suggestions, not a list of commandments.

Learn what you can, apply what you like, disregard what you don't like, and experiment.

Just remember, your story doesn't fit the universal plot skeleton . . . the universal plot skeleton fits your story.

And above all never forget the most essential universal plot skeleton of them all: **adversity builds character!**

~AUTHOR'S REMINDER~

If you enjoyed this book then please do me the fantastic favor of giving it an honest review on Amazon.com as well as sharing it with others. Thank you for your time.

~Adron J. Smitley

Pen the Sword Amazon customer review link:

http://www.Amazon.com/gp/customer-reviews/write-a-review.html?asin=B07F37Yl2G

adronjsmitley.blogspot.com

Printed in Great Britain
by Amazon

27027295R00059